Columbia University

Contributions to Education

Teachers College Series

No. 476

AMS PRESS

NEW YORK

AN ANALYSIS OF THE SUPERVISORY ACTIVITIES AND TECHNIQUES OF THE ELEMENTARY SCHOOL TRAINING SUPERVISOR

IN STATE NORMAL SCHOOLS AND TEACHERS COLLEGES

By

HARRY N. FITCH, Ph.D.

Teachers College, Columbia University
Contributions to Education, No. 476

Bureau of Publications
Teachers College, Columbia University
NEW YORK CITY
1931

Library of Congress Cataloging in Publication Data

Fitch, Harry Norton, 1887-
  An analysis of the supervisory activities and
techniques of the elementary school training supervisor
in state normal schools and teachers colleges.

  Reprint of the 1931 ed., issued in series: Teachers
College, Columbia University. Contributions to
education, no. 476.
  Originally presented as the author's thesis, Columbia.
  Bibliography: p.
  1. Elementary school teachers, Training of--United
States. 2. Teaching. I. Title. II. Series:
Columbia University. Teachers College. Contributions
to education, no. 476.

LB1731.F5 1972   370'.73262'0973   74-176774
ISBN 0-404-55476-8

Reprinted by Special Arrangement with Teachers
College Press, New York, New York

From the edition of 1931, New York
First AMS edition published in 1972
Manufactured in the United States

AMS PRESS, INC.
NEW YORK, N. Y.   10003

ACKNOWLEDGMENTS

It is a privilege to be able to express my appreciation of the encouragement and help given me by Professors Thomas Alexander, E. S. Evenden, F. G. Bonser, and W. C. Bagley, members of my dissertation committee. I am also most grateful to the large group of supervisors of student teaching who gave so freely of their time and energy in checking the activities listed in the check list. I owe much to Fannie Foote Fitch for her never failing encouragement and ever ready help.

H. N. F.

CONTENTS

CHAPTER I

INTRODUCTION AND PROBLEM

There is a rapidly growing body of literature dealing with the problems of teacher training. A thorough examination of this literature reveals, however, but few studies dealing specifically with the work of the laboratory schools of the teacher-training institutions and with the duties of the laboratory school workers. In 1927 Armentrout[1] made a study of the conduct of student teaching in which he reports 194 activities engaged in by student teachers. For grouping these activities he defined three types[2] of student teaching activities: (1) activities involving mechanical skill; (2) activities of a more complex nature which can be learned best in the actual student teaching situation; (3) activities of a still more complex nature which require considerable experience in teaching to be mastered. In the same year, Garrison[3] made a study of the status and work of the training supervisor, one section of which he devoted to a presentation of current practices in training supervision. This section[4] of his study reports the practices used by training supervisors in carrying on demonstration and observation teaching, participation, and practice teaching. Uhler,[5] in 1928, published a study dealing with the duties of the critic teacher. He used the check list technique and secured from critic teachers a list of 932 duties which they performed in carrying on their work. His findings are of value, but for the most part they are limited to one state. Charters and Waples,[6] in 1929, made a study of teacher training in which they report a comparison between the activities of student teachers in

---

[1] Armentrout, W. D., *Conduct of Student Teaching in State Teachers Colleges,* Chap. III. Colorado State Teachers College, Greeley, Colorado. 1927.

[2] *Ibid.*, p. 39.

[3] Garrison, Noble Lee, *Status and Work of the Training Supervisor.* Teachers College, Columbia University, Contributions to Education, No. 280, 1927.

[4] *Ibid.*, Chap. VI.

[5] Uhler, Joseph M., *A Partial Analysis of the Duties of the Critic Teacher.* Master's thesis, University of Pittsburgh, 1928.

[6] Charters, W. W. and Waples, Douglas, *The Commonwealth Teacher-Training Study,* pp. 30–34, University of Chicago Press, 1929.

a city training school and the activities of regularly employed city teachers. This comparison shows the following points: (1) The activities performed most frequently by experienced teachers are in general performed most frequently by student teachers also; (2) the activities performed by student teachers, however, tend to be limited to the teaching of subject matter, while the activities performed by experienced teachers include also duties relating to extra-curricular activities, community contacts, and the school plant and supplies; (3) many activities regarded as difficult to perform by experienced teachers are regarded as easy to perform by student teachers. All these studies have much of value to contribute to persons interested in the teacher-training program. They are of special interest and value to those who direct the work of the laboratory school that it may serve the needs of prospective teachers.

In the past ten years the enrollment in state normal schools and teachers colleges has been increasing very rapidly, with a consequent demand for greater and better laboratory facilities. Normal schools and teachers colleges are meeting this demand by establishing relations with public school authorities so as to have the use of the public schools for the training work. The result is that public school teachers, with no specific training, are undertaking the supervision of student teaching, a work which should be placed only in the hands of skilled and experienced teachers who have been trained specially for it.

Originally the laboratory school of a teacher-training institution was organized for the purpose of providing opportunities for student teaching. Too often, even at present, it has but this one purpose. More recently, however, it is coming to have the additional purpose of giving faculty and students an opportunity to see concretely and in actual use with children the best teaching materials and methods. To serve these ends the laboratory school must be staffed with skilled and experienced teachers of children, who, in addition, are specifically trained to join forces with the normal school or teachers college in organizing and maintaining a laboratory school which exemplifies teaching procedures and uses of materials that are in keeping with the best educational theory and practice. Such, briefly, are the reasons for making an analysis of the supervisory activities and techniques of the supervisor of student teaching.

The purpose of this study, broadly stated, is twofold:

1. To determine and analyze the activities of the elementary school training supervisor in working with student teachers.
2. To determine and analyze the techniques of the elementary school training supervisor in carrying on these activities.

It is believed that the study will be of aid in defining what should be the work of the supervisor of student teaching. Clearer definition should enable directors of training to make the work easier and more effective. The study also should furnish directors of training with information which may be used as a job specification in selecting training supervisors. Its chief value to directors of training, however, will probably result from their using the information obtained as a basis for a program of in-service improvement of elementary school training supervisors. The information obtained may be used by institutions of higher learning also in planning professional courses designed to prepare elementary school training supervisors.

CHAPTER II

METHOD OF PROCEDURE AND DATA

PREPARATION OF CHECK LIST

The check list was chosen as the best means of securing the information needed to accomplish the first purpose of the study. It was apparent at once that the training supervisor performs many activities which are commonly performed by all teachers of children. It was evident that these activities lay outside the scope of this study. It was decided, therefore, that the check list should be limited to the supervisory activities performed by the training supervisor, i.e., those activities which belong specifically to the training supervisor and not to the teacher who works only with children.

The following sources were examined to discover all possible activities that have been or might be performed by training supervisors in carrying on their work with student teachers:

1. Manuals of observation, participation, and student teaching.
2. Articles describing student teaching programs.
3. Reports of studies of laboratory schools for preparation of teachers.

The most fruitful source of supervisory activities found was Uhler's *Partial Analysis of the Duties of the Critic Teacher*, which, with Mr. Uhler's permission, has been used freely in this study.

Each activity found was listed separately on a card. It soon became evident that some classification of the activities had to be devised. After trial the following classification was devised:

1. Supervisory Activities Relating to Children.
2. Supervisory Activities Relating to Student Teachers.
3. Supervisory Activities Relating to Teaching.
4. Supervisory Activities Relating to School and Classroom Management.

4

    5. Supervisory Activities Relating to Administration of Student Teaching Program.

    6. Miscellaneous Supervisory Activities.

This classification has been adhered to throughout the study and is the one used in the check list.

Care was taken in wording the statement of each activity before recording it in its final form in the check list. The statements of the activities were submitted from time to time to training supervisors attending Teachers College, Columbia University, to insure a wording which would admit of but one interpretation. The training supervisors checking the wording also suggested additional activities. A total of 422 supervisory activities was finally secured. Of these, 70 relate to children, 70 to student teachers, 138 to teaching, 77 to school and classroom management, 35 to administration of student teaching program, and 32 are miscellaneous activities.

Instructions[1] for checking these 422 supervisory activities were prepared so as to secure a checking of each activity from the standpoint of three criteria: (1) frequency of performance; (2) need for specific training in activity before undertaking its performance; (3) value of the activity in the training of the student teacher.

Submitting of Check List

When the check list was completed, it was immediately apparent that to check it would require a considerable amount of time and effort on the part of the individual training supervisor. The writer went over the check list carefully, giving each piece of information asked for and checking all the activities according to the instructions. Although he had the advantage of being familiar with every point in the check list, to check it required 2 hours and 35 minutes. It was obvious that only those interested in the results of the study would take the time to give the information desired.

At the outset of the study it was decided to submit the check list personally to training supervisors in a limited number of schools, and by mail to training supervisors in a larger number of schools. It was desired also that the coöperating schools be so distributed that the information obtained should be fairly repre-

[1] See Appendix A for complete check list of supervisory activities and instructions.

sentative of the practices throughout the country as a whole. Accordingly there was prepared a list of eighty-four schools representing the whole country, whose chief executives and directors of training, it was thought, would be interested in the study. Two letters were sent out, one to the schools to be visited and the other to the schools to be communicated with by mail. These letters explained, in some detail, the purpose of the study and just what help was needed by the author. A very cordial response was received.

Ten normal schools and teachers colleges[2] in four states were visited. Personal interviews were held with several supervisors in each school and their help was secured in checking the activities of the check list. The help of training supervisors in thirty-five additional normal schools and teachers colleges in twenty-four states was obtained by mail. To the visited group of schools, 216 check lists were distributed. Of these, 119 check lists, or 55.0 per cent, were returned. To the mailed group of schools, 563 check lists were distributed. Of these, 262 check lists, or 46.5 per cent, were returned. Because of failure to follow directions and incomplete checking, 28 check lists could not be used, but of the total 779 check lists which were distributed there were returned 355 completed and usable check lists, or 45.5 per cent. These were distributed throughout the United States, as shown by Table I, and should be representative of the country as a whole.

TABLE I

DISTRIBUTION OF COÖPERATING TRAINING SUPERVISORS AND SCHOOLS AS TO NUMBER OF STATES AND SECTIONS OF THE COUNTRY*

SECTION OF UNITED STATES	NUMBER OF TRAINING SUPERVISORS	NUMBER OF SCHOOLS	NUMBER OF STATES
Northeastern	130	11	5
Southern	40	10	8
North Central	159	17	10
Western	26	7	5
Whole country	355	45	28

* For a list of the schools whose training supervisors coöperated in the study, see Appendix B.

[2] Three additional schools, each in a different state, were visited. Their training supervisors were engaged in a special piece of work at the time and could not coöperate in the study.

RELIABILITY OF DATA

To determine whether sufficient returns had been received to justify making conclusions concerning the ratings of the activities from the standpoint of the three criteria—(1) frequency of performance, (2) need for training, and (3) value to the student teacher—the correlation technique was used. Coefficients of correlation were computed between the ratings of the 422 activities of the check list based on each criterion by two representative groups of twenty primary grade training supervisors each. Similarly, coefficients of correlation were computed between ratings of the activities by two representative groups of intermediate grade training supervisors, and between ratings by two representative groups of grammar grade training supervisors. Each intermediate grade group consisted of twenty training supervisors, and each grammar grade group consisted of twenty-two training supervisors. These coefficients of correlation are shown in Table II. All are significantly high and warrant the conclusion that sufficient returns have been received for the purpose of the study.

TABLE II

COEFFICIENTS OF CORRELATION BETWEEN RATINGS OF ACTIVITIES BASED ON SAME CRITERION BY REPRESENTATIVE GROUPS OF TRAINING SUPERVISORS

CRITERION*	PRIMARY TRAINING SUPERVISORS		INTERMEDIATE TRAINING SUPERVISORS		GRAMMAR TRAINING SUPERVISORS	
	r	P.E.	r	P.E.	r	P.E.
Frequency of performance	.882	± .007	.895	± .006	.880	± .007
Need for training	.761	± .013	.790	± .012	.785	± .012
Value to student teacher	.790	± .012	.824	± .010	.861	± .008

* For statement of the criteria as given to training supervisors, see Appendix A, p. 79.

DISCRETENESS OF CRITERIA

Coefficients of correlation were computed also between ratings of the activities based on one criterion and ratings based on each of the other two criteria. These ratings are the same as those used to show the reliability of the data of this study. The coefficients of correlation obtained are shown in Table III. The r's between ratings based on the first criterion and ratings based on the second criterion, and between ratings based on the second criterion and ratings based on the third criterion are in no case higher than .540 ± .022. Apparently each of these criteria has a distinct meaning of its own in the judgment of the training supervisors. The *r's* between ratings based on the first criterion and ratings based on the third criterion are significantly high, however, the lowest being .751 ± .014. This rather high relationship between these ratings does not necessarily mean that the first and third criteria are not discrete. Instead, it may mean that the training supervisors are able to judge what activities are of value in the training of the student teacher, and so they perform these activities frequently in their work.

TABLE III

COEFFICIENTS OF CORRELATION BETWEEN RATINGS OF ACTIVITIES BASED ON DIFFERENT CRITERIA BY REPRESENTATIVE GROUPS OF TRAINING SUPERVISORS

CRITERIA*	PRIMARY TRAINING SUPERVISORS		INTERMEDIATE TRAINING SUPERVISORS		GRAMMAR TRAINING SUPERVISORS	
	r	*P.E.*	*r*	*P.E.*	*r*	*P.E.*
1 and 2	.368	± .028	.313	± .029	.267	± .030
1 and 3	.760	± .013	.751	± .014	.810	± .011
2 and 3	.540	± .022	.458	± .025	.449	± .026

* Criterion 1 is frequency of performance; criterion 2 is need for training; criterion 3 is value to the student teacher.

As a check on those *r's* of Table III which are .540 ± .022 or lower eta was computed also. The reason for doing this was suggested by the nonlinear appearance of the scatterdiagrams used in computing the *r's*. The correlation ratios found are shown in Table IV. In no case is the correlation ratio, or eta, higher than .548 ± .022.

The facts that the coefficients of correlation between ratings based on the same criteria are high and that coefficients of correlation between ratings based on different criteria are relatively lower tend to show that the criteria are discrete and that their use in this study is valid.

TABLE IV

CORRELATION RATIOS (ETA)* BETWEEN RATINGS OF ACTIVITIES BASED ON
DIFFERENT CRITERIA BY REPRESENTATIVE GROUPS OF
TRAINING SUPERVISORS

CRITERIA†	PRIMARY TRAINING SUPERVISORS		INTERMEDIATE TRAINING SUPERVISORS		GRAMMAR TRAINING SUPERVISORS	
	η	*P.E.*	η	*P.E.*	η	*P.E.*
1 and 2	.401	± .027	.388	± .027	.345	± .029
2 and 3	.548	± .022	.517	± .024	.480	± .025

* Blakeman's test for linearity indicates that the relation between the first and second criteria, and between the second and third criteria tends to be nonlinear.

† Criterion 1 is frequency of performance; criterion 2 is need for training; criterion 3 is value to the student teacher.

SUMMARY

To determine the supervisory activities performed by elementary school training supervisors in their work with student teachers, a check list of 422 activities was prepared. This check list was submitted personally by the writer to training supervisors in ten normal schools and teachers colleges and through the mail to training supervisors in thirty-five additional normal schools and teachers colleges. A total of 779 check lists was distributed, and of these 355 completed and usable check lists were returned, or 45.5 per cent.

Training supervisors were asked to check the supervisory activities from the standpoint of three criteria: (1) frequency of performance of activity in work with student teacher; (2) need for training in activity before undertaking its performance in work with student teacher; (3) value of activity in the training of student teacher.

Coefficients of correlation computed between ratings of the activities based on the same criterion by representative groups of training supervisors are significantly high, ranging from .761 ± .013 to .895 ± .006. These *r*'s warrant the conclusion that the ratings secured were sufficiently reliable for the purpose of the study.

Coefficients of correlation computed between ratings of the activities based on different criteria by representative groups of training supervisors are lower. In the case of the relation between the first and second criteria the coefficients range, for r, from .267 ± .030 to .368 ± .028, and, for eta, from .345 ± .029 to .401 ± .027. In the case of the relation between the second and third criteria the coefficients range, for r, from .449 ± .026 to .540 ± .022, and, for eta, from .480 ± .025 to .548 ± .022. In the case of the relation between the first and third criteria the $r's$ range from .751 ± .014 to .810 ± .011. The rather high relation between the first and third criteria may mean that training supervisors perform frequently those activities that are of value to the student teacher. The rather low relations between the first and second criteria and between the second and third criteria indicate that the criteria are discrete and that their use in the study is valid.

CHAPTER III

ANALYSIS OF TRAINING AND EXPERIENCE OF TRAINING SUPERVISORS

Judgments of any group of workers with respect to any question relating to their work obviously are influenced by the amount and kind of training and experience the workers have had. Because of this fact, the training supervisors rating the activities of the check list were asked to give certain information relating to their training and experience.

From the standpoint of their training, the training supervisors were asked to give: (1) length of training and type of institution in which training was taken; (2) names of courses taken which had been of specific help in work with student teachers; (3) suggestions as to name and content of courses which might have been taken with profit prior to undertaking work with student teachers.

From the standpoint of their experience, the training supervisors were asked to give: (1) length of total teaching experience and of experience as training supervisor; (2) total number of student teachers supervised and number of student teachers being supervised at the time of filling out the check list; (3) types of teaching positions held and length of stay in each; (4) type of position held at the time of filling out the check list and whether in a campus training school or in a public school affiliated for training purposes.

The purpose of this chapter is to present the information relating to training and experience and to show its bearing on the study.

TRAINING

1. The facts relating to types of institutions attended, length of training taken, and highest diploma or degree earned by the 355 training supervisors are shown in Tables V, VI, and VII.

Study of Table V shows that 320 training supervisors, or 90.1 per cent of the group contributing data for this study, had attended normal school or teachers college, the median length of such attendance being 2.7 years. Furthermore, 151, or 42.5 per cent, had attended summers at normal school or teachers college, the median length of such attendance being 3.1 summers. This means that the training supervisors had had experience as students in the same type of institution in which they later served as super-

TABLE V

Types of Institutions Attended by 355 Training Supervisors and Median Number of Years and Summers Attended in Each

NUMBER OF YEARS OR SUMMERS	NUMBER OF TRAINING SUPERVISORS ATTENDING					
	Normal School or Teachers College		College		University	
	Year	Summer	Year	Summer	Year	Summer
1	37	38	16	22	42	45
2	180	36	20	15	28	36
3	38	25	7	9	14	28
4	59	12	13	4	15	17
5	5	10	1	1	2	5
6	..	9	..	..	1	4
7	1	21	..	2	..	3
Total	320	151	57	53	102	138
Per cent of group .	90.1	42.5	16.1	14.0	28.7	38.9
Median attendance	2.7	3.1	2.6	2.3	2.3	2.7

Note: The table reads: Of the 355 supervisors, 37 attended normal school or teachers college one year and 38 attended normal school or teachers college one summer; 16 attended college one year and 22 attended college one summer; 42 attended university one year and 45 attended university one summer, etc. The bottom of the table reads: Of the 355 supervisors, 320, or 90.1 per cent, attended normal school or teachers college during the regular school year, the median length of such attendance being 2.7 years; 151 or 42.5 per cent, attended normal school or teachers college during summers, the median length of such attendance being 3.1 summers; etc.

visors. This would undoubtedly have proved unfortunate had they taken no further training, but 44.8 per cent of the group had attended college and university during the regular school year, the median length of such attendance being better than 2 years, and 52.9 per cent had attended college and university during summers, the median length of such attendance being more than 2 summers.

Table VI shows the amount of training beyond high school

taken by the 355 training supervisors. In making Table VI, four summers were considered equivalent to one year.

TABLE VI

AMOUNT OF TRAINING BEYOND HIGH SCHOOL TAKEN
BY 355 SUPERVISORS

NUMBER OF YEARS	TRAINING SUPERVISORS	
	Number	Per Cent
1	8	2.3
2	111	31.3
3	58	16.3
4	99	27.9
5	40	11.3
6	25	7.0
7	9	2.5
8	4	1.1
9	1	0.3
Total	355	100.0
Median	4.0	

Note: The table reads: Of the 355 supervisors, 8, or 2.3 per cent, had had one year of training beyond high school; etc.

Table VI shows that approximately one-half of the supervisors had had 3 years or less of training beyond high school and one-half had had 4 years or more of training beyond high school. The median number of years of training beyond high school is 4.0 years, with a gross range from 1 year of training for eight supervisors to 9 years of training for one.

The facts relating to highest diploma or degree earned by the 355 supervisors are shown in Table VII. It is interesting to note that, while but 178 of the supervisors (Table VI) had taken 4 years or more of training beyond high school, 182 had earned the bachelor's or a higher degree. This indicates that the supervisors when taking advanced training had been making efforts to meet degree requirements.

The training supervisors contributing data for this study do not seem to be trained so well as were those contributing to Garrison's study.[1] Of the training supervisors studied by Garrison,

[1] Garrison, Noble Lee, *Status and Work of the Training Supervisor*, Chap. II. Teachers College, Columbia University, Contributions to Education, No. 280, 1927.

TABLE VII

HIGHEST DIPLOMA OR DEGREE FOR TRAINING BEYOND HIGH SCHOOL
EARNED BY 355 SUPERVISORS

DIPLOMA OR DEGREE	TRAINING SUPERVISORS	
	Number	Per Cent
Two-year normal school diploma	173	48.7
Normal school or teachers college bachelor's degree	65	18.3
College bachelor's degree	15	4.2
University bachelor's degree	57	16.1
Teachers college master's degree	1	0.3
College master's degree	4	1.1
University master's degree	38	10.7
University doctor's degree	2	0.6
Total	355	100.0

64.0 per cent of the women and 80.0 per cent of the men held the bachelor's degree. Of the training supervisors of this study, 49.9 per cent had had less than 4 years of training, 50.1 per cent had had 4 years of training or more, and 51.2 per cent held degrees. This difference may be due to the fact that all the training supervisors of this study were working in the elementary grades where the standard period of training for teachers is but 2 years in length. In connection with this fact it must be remembered that 61.9 per cent of the training supervisors of this study were working in affiliated public schools and not in the campus training school. (Table XVI.)

2. Of the 355 training supervisors who rated the activities of the check list, 300 reported names of courses taken which had given them specific help in their work with student teachers. The names of the courses so reported are given in Table VIII.

These additional courses were mentioned once by a training supervisor as having been of specific help in work with student teachers: Abnormal Psychology, Administration of Normal Schools and Teachers Colleges, Child Welfare, Course in Nursing, Creative Education, Dramatic Presentation, Extra-Curricular Activities, Free Art for the Grades, Improvement of Written Examinations, Mental Hygiene, Methods in Industrial Arts, Music, Music Methods, Poetry Appreciation, Problems of the High

School Teacher Training Department, Psychiatry, Psychology of Personality, Research in Student Teaching, Research in Supervision, Story Telling, Supervision of Moral Education, Supervision of Teaching of Art, Supervision of Teaching of History, Supervision of Teaching of Industrial Arts, Supervision of Teaching of Language and Literature, Supervision of Teaching of Music, Teaching of Hygiene, and Vocational Guidance.

Training supervisors differ in their ability to analyze their training with a view to picking out those elements which may be of specific help to them in their work with student teachers. This is revealed in the information given by the training supervisors in response to the request for names of courses taken which had been of specific help to them in their work with student teachers.

One training supervisor, in reply to the request for names of courses taken which had given her specific help in her work, wrote:

"These seem to be lacking."

This reply was made by a training supervisor who had completed 2 years of training at a normal school, had attended summer school at a college for 1 summer and at a university for 3 summers, and had had 6 years of experience as classroom teacher and 8½ years of experience as training supervisor. In contrast to this reply is the reply made by another training supervisor,

"I do not recall any course I have taken which has not had some specific value to me at some time in my work with student teachers. Of general educational courses, I probably use most educational psychology, principles of education, curriculum construction, and tests and measurements. Courses which keep me up to date in the subject matter I teach are very vital to me."

This second training supervisor had completed 4 years of training in a teachers college leading to the bachelor's degree, had attended a university for 2 quarters and 1 summer, and had had 16 years of experience as classroom teacher and 17 years of experience as training supervisor.

It may be that a great many training supervisors interpreted too literally the request for names of courses taken which had given specific help. Evidence for this is suggested by the fact that, of the 355 training supervisors filling out the check list, 55

TABLE VIII

NAMES OF COURSES TAKEN BY 300 TRAINING SUPERVISORS WHICH HAD
GIVEN SPECIFIC HELP IN WORK WITH STUDENT TEACHERS

NAME OF COURSE	FREQUENCY OF MENTION
Supervision of Instruction	157
Supervision of Student Teaching	77
Educational Psychology	61
Tests and Measurements	51
Methods	38
Student Teaching	35
School Administration	33
Child Psychology	31
Directed Observation	31
Principles of Education	25
Classroom Management	24
Technique of Teaching	24
Principles of Teaching	23
Primary Education	22
Curriculum Construction	21
Reading Methods and Materials	19
Elementary Education	16
Foundations of Method	15
Teaching of Arithmetic	14
Philosophy of Education	13
Training School Problems	13
Methods in English	11
Psychology of Elementary School Subjects	11
Professional Education of Teachers	11
English	11
Methods in Common Branches	10
Supervision of Teaching of Reading	9
Research for Teachers	7
Art and Handwork for the Grades	7
Problems of the Junior High School	7
Adolescent Psychology	7
Teaching of Literature in the Grades	7
Industrial Arts for the Grades	6
History of Education	6
Social Studies for the Grades	6
Supervision of Teaching of Arithmetic	6
Experimental Education	6
Kindergarten-Primary Methods	6
Methods in History	5
Methods in Geography	5
Sociology	5
Introduction to Education	5
Subject Matter Courses (See note at end of table)	5
Methods of Teaching for Experienced Teachers and Supervisors	4
Experimental Psychology	4

TABLE VIII—(*Continued*)

Name of Course	Frequency of Mention
Teaching of English	4
Psychology of Individual Differences	4
Practice in Supervision	4
Supervision of Teaching of Geography	4
Educational Sociology	4
Projects and Project Method	4
Science for the Elementary School	4
Teaching Exceptional Children	4
Supervision of Play and Games	3
Supervision of the Social Studies	3
Teaching How to Study	3
Activities of Primary Grades	3
Americanization	3
Physical Education	3
Application of Psychology to Teaching	2
Character Education	2
Literature in the Elementary School	2
Geography	2
Folk Dancing	2
Modern Tendencies in Education	2
Methods in the Special Subjects	2
United States History	2
Educational Statistics	2
Visual Education	2
Vocational Psychology	2
Teaching of Spelling	2

Note: Five training supervisors reported subject matter courses as having given help in their work without mentioning any particular one.

mention no course which had been of specific help to them in their work with student teachers. Of the 300 training supervisors who do mention helpful courses, 38 mention but one course each. The courses mentioned by these 38 training supervisors, together with the frequency of mention, are as follows: Supervision of Student Teaching, 19; Supervision of Instruction, 17; Student Teaching, 2. It is certain that these training supervisors had received specific help from many other courses.

Examination of Table VIII shows the same tendency to mention as most helpful only those courses dealing with problems of supervision of instruction and supervision of student teaching. In this table the names of seventy-three courses, reported by training supervisors as being helpful, are arranged in order of frequency of mention.   Not until one reaches the sixteenth course reported in Table VIII—Reading Methods and Materials—does one find the first course which deals specifically with the materials and methods of one of the subjects of instruction. The nineteenth —Teaching of Arithmetic—is the next such course; the twenty-second—Methods in English—is the next such; and the twenty-sixth—English—is the fourth such course.   These four courses have the respective frequencies of 19, 14, 11, and 11.   The fact that, out of 300 training supervisors, fewer than 20 mention any one subject matter course as being of specific help in work with student teachers presents a distinct challenge to teachers of courses in supervision of instruction as well as to teachers of subject matter courses.   It is a distinct challenge to the former, because in the courses in supervision the principles given have not enabled the prospective supervisor to sense more clearly her best sources of help; to the latter, because their courses have not been organized and presented in such a way as to be of more apparent value to the prospective supervisor of student teachers.

These facts become even more clear when a grouping of the related courses given in Table VIII is made. Such a grouping is given in Table IX.   Study of Table IX with its low frequency of mention of courses dealing with subject matter bears testimony to the fact that we are very slow in organizing subject matter courses which the prospective teacher of children recognizes as being of direct value to her in her work with children.

3. Of the 355 training supervisors who rated the activities of

TABLE IX

GROUPING OF RELATED COURSES TAKEN BY 300 TRAINING SUPERVISORS WHICH HAD GIVEN SPECIFIC HELP IN WORK WITH STUDENT TEACHERS

COURSE GROUPS	FREQUENCY OF MENTION
Principles of Supervision	339
Principles of Education	219
Psychology	175
Methods	115
Subject Matter Courses	50
School Administration	40
Teaching of Subject Matter Courses	34

the check list, 200 suggested names of courses, and topics to be treated in the courses, which they wish they might have taken before undertaking the supervision of student teaching. The names of courses suggested are given in Table X. The topics

TABLE X

NAMES OF COURSES SUGGESTED BY 200 SUPERVISORS TO BE TAKEN PRIOR TO WORKING WITH STUDENT TEACHERS

NAME OF COURSE	FREQUENCY OF MENTION
Supervision of Student Teaching	99
Supervision of Instruction	10
Training School Problems	9
Evaluation of Student Teaching	9
Child Psychology (Case Studies)	6
Technique of Teaching	6
Directed Observation	4
Graded Units in Student Teaching	4
Personality Development	4
Primary Supervision	4
Projects and the Project Method	4
Research Study of Teaching in Public Schools	4
Practice Supervision for Training Supervisors	3
Psychology of Elementary School Subjects	3
Intelligence Testing	2
Professional Subject Matter Courses in Subjects Taught (Materials, Methods)	2
Remedial Teaching	1
Educational Psychology	1
Objectives in Modern Education	1
Organization and Function of Teachers Colleges	1

suggested for treatment in the courses reported in Table X are given in Table XI.[2]

In addition to the topics given in Table XI, these topics were reported once by a training supervisor: Analysis of speech difficulties of children and remedial treatment; how help student teacher develop a good teaching voice; how provide cultural experiences for the student teachers; how teach art as an illustrative medium for all subjects; study of the Dalton Plan; history of

[2] In preparing the lists of names of courses reported in Tables VIII and X and the lists of topics reported in Table XI considerable liberty has been taken with the wording used by the training supervisors when reporting these items. Great care has been taken by the writer, in changing the wording, to insure no change in meaning.

TABLE XI

Topic	Frequency of Mention
Conferences of training supervisor with student teacher	52
a. Study of the needs and interests of children	38
b. Psychological principles guiding training supervisor in criticism of student teacher	19
c. Helpful techniques and devices to suggest to student teacher	7
d. Discussion of professional ethics and standards	1
e. Definite program for conferences with student teachers	1
Curriculum construction	38
a. Selection and organization of subject matter for teaching	16
b. Correlation of subject matter	5
c. Psychological justification of subject matter selected	3
d. Study of community life, as a basis for project work	4
e. Study of reports of research dealing with teaching materials and methods	3
Rating of student teacher	35
a. Rating of student teacher by training supervisor	23
b. Self-rating of student teacher	6
c. Standards of attainment to be used by student teacher	26
Essentials of good supervision of student teaching	31
a. Graded introduction to responsible teaching	25
b. How start student teachers	5
c. How teach student teacher to observe	7
d. How keep student teacher growing	24
e. How develop initiative on part of student teacher	9
f. How keep a record of student teacher's progress	1
g. How make student teacher feel responsible for progress of pupils	5
h. How observe student teacher teach	3
i. When stop close supervision and permit student teacher to teach independently	1
j. A study of the objectives of teaching	5
k. Type lessons in various subjects	4
l. Criteria for judging type lessons	2
m. Analysis of the teaching act	5
n. Different methods for same teaching situation evaluated	3
o. Study of questioning	2
p. Diagnostic testing and remedial teaching	8
q. How stimulate creative work on part of children	6
r. Professional organization of subject matter (materials and methods)	4

TABLE XI (*Continued*)

Topic	Frequency of Mention
Application of psychology to work of training supervisor	25
a. Case studies of children	10
b. Case studies of student teachers	3
c. Psychology of learning	10
d. Psychology of thinking	2
Personality as a factor in teaching	22
a. Program for improvement of personality of student teachers	3
b. Case studies of success and failure in teaching due to personality	2
How meet individual needs of student teachers	22
a. Nature of preparation of student teachers before attempting student teaching	5
b. Survey of what student teachers want training supervisors to do for them	1
c. Report from student teachers of what experiences in their student teaching were of value to them	1
d. How teach student teacher how to study	3
Technique of teaching	16
a. Study of modern teaching practices with underlying psychological principles	10
Study of position and work of training supervisor	10
a. Relation of training supervisor to director of training ...	8
b. How make suggestions to director of training concerning problems to be discussed in general conferences with student teachers	2
c. Topics for conferences of director of training with training supervisors	1
d. Relation of training supervisors to normal school or teachers college	4
e. How coördinate theory taught in normal school or teachers college with practice of training school	3
f. Relation of training supervisor to student teacher	8
g. An organized view of valuable and necessary supervisory activities, determined by a study of the work in best public schools	5
h. What types of activities should each student teacher perform	2
i. Just how specific should the help given the student teacher be	2
j. How insure that student teaching experiences carry over to real teaching situations	1
k. Personality of successful training supervisor	3

TABLE XI (*Continued*)

Topic	Frequency of Mention
Bibliography for student teachers	12
Bibliography for training supervisors	10
Directed observation and discussion of lessons observed	8
Discipline problems	7
a. Helping student teacher control his pupils	1
b. Disciplining student teachers	1
Mental hygiene	6
Classroom management	5
Health education	2
Principles of education	2

normal schools and teachers colleges; vital problems confronting normal schools and teachers colleges; and the outlook confronting normal schools and teachers colleges. One training supervisor wants the opportunity to work, for a time, with a competent and experienced training supervisor and another wants to visit the college classes.

Table X, giving the suggested names of courses which supervisors wish they might have taken before undertaking the supervision of student teachers, presents much the same picture as do Tables VIII and IX. The same courses rank first in order of frequency in Table X as in Tables VIII and IX. In fact, it seems that teachers generally do not think that there might be subject matter courses which they wish they had taken prior to working with student teachers. Out of these 355 training supervisors only two mentioned the subject matter courses which they wish they had taken and they both emphasized that these courses should have been a professional treatment of the subject matter which they teach.

The topics which the training supervisors would have these courses (reported in Table X) treat give a clearer picture as to the training the training supervisors wish they had taken prior to working with student teachers. These topics are shown in Table XI. An examination of these topics shows that training supervisors, as a group, do see what their task is and that they are capable of suggesting the elements or parts of a program designed to prepare training supervisors. The study of these topics shows that experienced training supervisors advocate specific training for those desiring to supervise student teaching, and that this specific training should treat thoroughly these problems: (1) conferences of training supervisor with student teacher, (2) curriculum construction, (3) rating of student teachers, (4) essentials of good supervision of student teaching, (5) application of psychology to work of training supervisor, (6) personality as a factor in teaching, (7) how meet individual needs of student teachers, (8) technique of teaching, (9) study of the position and work of the training supervisor, (10) bibliographies for student teachers and training supervisors, (11) directed observation and discussion of lessons observed, (12) discipline problems, (13) mental hygiene, (14) classroom management, (15) health education, and (16) principles of education. Many other topics were advocated. For convenience these have been grouped under different ones of the sixteen larger topics and reported in Table XI. They show, in a measure, the detailed treatment which the training supervisors would wish to have given the larger topics. It should be noted that among these other topics are three which indicate an interest on the part of the supervisors in the subject matter which they teach. These topics are: (1) selection and organization of subject matter to be taught; (2) correlation of subject matter; (3) professional organization of subject matter. These topics have the respective frequencies of 16, 5, and 4. So little appreciation of the need of subject matter on the part of training supervisors presents a problem to those planning their training.

It is significant that four training supervisors advocated practice in supervision of student teachers as a part of the training which they wish they had taken before undertaking the supervision of student teachers. This is indicated in Table X, in which the course Practice Supervision for Training Supervisors is recorded with a frequency of 3, and in one of the single topics enumerated following Table XI. This one topic—opportunity to work with a well-trained and experienced training supervisor for a period— was reported by a training supervisor who had completed 4 years of training in a teachers college leading to the bachelor's degree, had attended university for 1 summer, and had had 2 years of experience as a classroom teacher and 3 years of experience as a training supervisor.

EXPERIENCE

1. The facts relating to length of total experience in school work and to length of experience in supervision of student teaching are given in Table XII. Of the 353 training supervisors

TABLE XII

TOTAL SCHOOL EXPERIENCE AND TRAINING SUPERVISION EXPERIENCE OF 353 TRAINING SUPERVISORS *

NUMBER OF YEARS	NUMBER OF TRAINING SUPERVISORS	
	Having Total School Experience	Having Training Supervision Experience
1– 3	22	145
4– 6	43	103
7– 9	43	46
10–12	52	21
13–15	64	3
16–18	42	12
19–21	29	10
22–24	15	4
25–27	16	2
28–30	12	2
31–33	4	4
34–36	5	..
37–39	2	..
40–	4	1
Total	353	353
Median	13.8	4.9

Note: The table reads: Of 353 training supervisors, 22 have had from 1 to 3 years of experience in school work and 145 have had from 1 to 3 years of experience as a training supervisor, etc.

* Two training supervisors did not report the information given in Table XII.

reporting this information, 22, or 6.2 per cent, had had from 1 to 3 years of experience in school work while 43, or 12.2 per cent, had had from 25 to 40 years of experience in school work. On the other hand, 145, or 41.1 per cent, had had from 1 to 3 years of experience in supervision of student teaching, while 9, or 2.5 per cent, had had from 25 to 40 years of experience in supervision of student teaching. The median length of total school experience for the group is 13.8 years and the median length of experience in supervision of student teaching is 4.9 years. These data show that the training supervisors were experienced teachers before they undertook the supervision of student teaching.

2. With respect to the total number of student teachers supervised and the number of student teachers being supervised by the training supervisors at the time of filling out the check list, the facts are shown in Table XIII. Study of Table XIII shows that 70, or 20.6 per cent, of the 339 training supervisors reporting this information had supervised from 1 to 20 student teachers. Of the 339 supervisors, 129, or 38.0 per cent, were supervising from 0 to 2 student teachers at the time the data for this study

TABLE XIII

TOTAL NUMBER OF STUDENT TEACHERS SUPERVISED AND NUMBER BEING SUPERVISED BY 339 TRAINING SUPERVISORS WHEN DATA WERE COLLECTED *

TOTAL NUMBER OF STUDENT TEACHERS SUPERVISED	TRAINING SUPERVISORS	NUMBER OF STUDENT TEACHERS BEING SUPERVISED WHEN DATA WERE COLLECTED	TRAINING SUPERVISORS
1– 10	30	0	13
11– 20	40	1– 2	116
21– 30	29	3– 4	40
31– 40	30	5– 6	53
41– 50	20	7– 8	34
51– 60	12	9–10	19
61– 70	6	11–12	12
71– 80	15	13–14	7
81– 90	8	15–16	4
91–100	9	17–18	7
101–110	5	19–20	9
111–120	4	21–22	3
121–130	8	23–24	4
131–140	4	25–26	1
141–150	14	27–28	1
151–160	1	29–30	1
161–170	1	31–32	1
171–180	4	33–34	..
181–190	1	35–36	1
191–200	3	37–38	1
200–	95	39–	12
Total	339	Total	339
Median	72.7	Median	5.0

Note: The table reads: Of 339 training supervisors, 30 had supervised a total of from 1 to 10 student teachers and 13 were supervising no student teachers when the data for the study were collected; etc.

* Sixteen training supervisors did not report the information given in Table XIII.

were collected. These data indicate that a rather large number of the supervisors had had a somewhat limited experience in supervision of student teaching. On the other hand, a large number had had an extended and rich experience, the median total number of student teachers supervised being 72.7 and the median number being supervised at the time the data for the study were collected being 5.0.

3. With respect to the kinds of teaching experience the training supervisors had had prior to undertaking supervision of student teaching the facts are shown in Table XIV. This table shows that the supervisors, as a group, had experienced successfully all

TABLE XIV

KINDS OF SCHOOL EXPERIENCE PRIOR TO UNDERTAKING SUPERVISION OF STUDENT TEACHING AND LENGTH OF SUCH EXPERIENCE AS REPORTED BY 351 TRAINING SUPERVISORS *

EXPERIENCE AS	NUMBER REPORTING	PER CENT REPORTING	MEDIAN YEARS OF EXPERIENCE
Kindergarten—primary teacher	164	46.7	5.2
Intermediate teacher	121	34.5	4.1
Grammar teacher	73	20.8	4.1
Rural school teacher	103	29.3	3.0
Junior high school teacher	22	6.3	3.0
Senior high school teacher	45	12.8	3.3
Elementary school principal	22	6.3	3.2
Junior high school principal	4	1.1	3.5
Senior high school principal	13	3.7	3.5
County superintendent	1	0.3	2.0
City superintendent	13	3.7	4.7
Teachers college teacher	11	3.1	3.3
College or university teacher	9	2.6	2.0

Note: The table reads: Of 351 training supervisors, 164, or 46.7 per cent, had had experience in kindergarten-primary teaching, the median length of such experience being 5.2 years; etc.
* Four training supervisors did not report the information given in Table XIV.

types of teaching, from kindergarten-primary to college and university teaching, and that they had served successfully as principals of elementary, junior high, and senior high schools and as city and county superintendents of schools. The median length of the school experience prior to undertaking supervision of student teaching is 8.9 years. The median length of experience in supervision of student teaching is 4.9 years.

4. The facts with respect to the type of position held by the training supervisors at the time of filling out the check list and whether in a campus training school or in a public school, affiliated for training purposes, are shown in Tables XV and XVI. Table XV shows that approximately 75 per cent of the training supervisors reported in this study were working in the first six grades, 20 per cent were working in the grammar grades, and 5 per cent were directors or assistant directors of training. Table XVI shows that 131 training supervisors, or 36.9 per cent, were working in campus training schools, that 220, or 61.9 per cent, were working in affiliated public schools, and that 5, or 1.4 per cent, were working in both campus training schools and affiliated public schools. The fact that more than half of the training supervisors

TABLE XV

TYPE OF POSITION HELD AS REPORTED BY 355 TRAINING SUPERVISORS

TYPE OF POSITION	NUMBER OF SUPERVISORS	PERCENTAGE OF SUPERVISORS
Primary	138	38.9
Intermediate	125	35.2
Grammar	73	20.5
Director of training	19	5.4

Note: The table reads: Of 355 training supervisors, 138, or 38.9 per cent, are training supervisors in Grades 1, 2, and 3, etc.

were working in affiliated public schools may indicate that, at the time the data were collected, the majority of student teachers were having their training in the actual public school situation rather than in the campus training school.

TABLE XVI

TYPE OF SCHOOL IN WHICH THE 355 TRAINING SUPERVISORS WERE WORKING

TYPE OF SCHOOL	NUMBER OF SUPERVISORS	PERCENTAGE OF SUPERVISORS
Campus school	131	36.7
Affiliated public school	219	61.8
Campus and affiliated public school	5	1.4

Summary

The important facts relating to the training and experience of the 355 training supervisors whose ratings of the activities of the check list constitute an important part of the data of this study are:

1. Approximately 50.0 per cent of the training supervisors had had less than 4 years of training and 50.0 per cent had had 4 years or more of training. Approximately 50.0 per cent held the normal school or teachers college diploma representing 2 years of work as their highest diploma; 18.3 per cent held the bachelor's degree granted by a teachers college, 4.2 per cent held the bachelor's degree granted by a college, and 16.1 per cent held the bachelor's degree granted by a university as their highest degree; 1 held the master's degree granted by a teachers college, 4 held the master's degree granted by a college, and 38 held the master's degree granted by a university, making a total of 12.1 per cent who held the master's degree as their highest degree; 2 held the doctor's degree granted by a university.

2. Training supervisors interpreted too literally, perhaps, the request for names of courses taken which had given specific help in work with student teachers. Courses mentioned most frequently as having given specific help are courses in supervision and psychology, while courses dealing with materials and methods of the subject matter of instruction were mentioned relatively infrequently. The contention is made that this situation presents a distinct challenge to the teacher of courses in supervision for not having developed principles of supervision in such a way as to enable the prospective supervisor to sense more clearly her best sources of help, and to the teacher of the subject matter courses for not having organized and presented these courses in such a way as to. be of more value to the prospective supervisor.

3. The topics suggested by the training supervisor for treatment in courses which might have been taken profitably prior to undertaking work with student teachers show that training supervisors, as a group, are able to make valuable suggestions with respect to a program of training designed to meet the needs of training supervisors.

4. The training supervisors, as a group, were experienced school people. The median length of total school experience is 13.8

years, with a gross range of from 1 to 40 years. The median length of experience in supervision of student teaching is 4.9 years, with a gross range of from 1 to 40 years.

5. Training supervisors, as a group, had had a rich and extended experience in supervising student teaching, the median total number of student teachers supervised being 72.7 and the median number being supervised at the time the data for this study were collected being 5.0.

6. The data relating to experience show that the training supervisors had experienced successfully all types of teaching, from kindergarten to university teaching, and had served successfully in all phases of public school administrative work prior to undertaking the supervision of student teaching. The median length of this experience is 8.9 years. The median length of experience as training supervisor is 4.9 years.

These facts of training and experience for the 355 training supervisors qualify them, as a group, to register valuable judgments with respect to questions relating to their work.

CHAPTER IV

ANALYSIS OF THE SUPERVISORY ACTIVITIES OF THE TRAINING SUPERVISORS

Decile Ranks of Activities

Tabulation of the ratings[1] by supervisors of student teachers of the activities of the check list shows (1) the total number of *performed frequently, performed less frequently, performed least frequently,* and *performed not at all* ratings, (2) the total number of *need for training* ratings, and (3) the total number of *better than average value, average value,* and *less than average value* ratings for each activity of the check list.

A composite frequency rating of each activity was made as follows: (1) A weighting scheme of 1 for all *performed frequently* ratings of the activity, of 2 for all *performed less frequently* ratings, of 3 for all *performed least frequently* ratings, and of 4 for all *performed not at all* ratings was used; (2) these weighted ratings were then totaled, giving the composite frequency rating for the activity. A composite rating of each activity for need for training was made by merely totaling the number of ratings indicating need for training. A composite rating of each activity for value to the student teacher was made as follows: (1) A weighting scheme of 1 for *better than average value* ratings of the activity; of 2 for all *average value* ratings; and of 3 for all *less than average value* ratings was used; (2) these weighted ratings were then totaled, giving the composite rating from the standpoint of value to the student teacher.[2]

---

[1] For instructions to supervisors for rating the activities see Appendix A, p. 79.

[2] An illustration is here given. The ratings of the first activity of the first section of the check list by the 355 training supervisors are as follows: (1) From the standpoint of frequency of performance—(a) performed frequently, 268; (b) performed less frequently, 46; (c) performed least frequently, 33; and (d) performed not at all, 8; (2) from the standpoint of need for training, 86; (3) from the standpoint of value to the student teacher—(a) of better than average value, 295; (b) of average value, 34; and (c) of less than average value, 26. When the weighting scheme described above is used and weighted ratings based on each criterion are totaled, the composite ratings for this particular activity become: (1) From the standpoint of frequency of performance, 491; (2) from the standpoint of need for training, 86; (3) from the standpoint of value to the student teacher, 441.

Decile ranks[3] of the activities of the entire check list according to each criterion were computed based upon the composite ratings. These decile ranks were numbered from 1 to 10, 1 being the lowest and 10 the highest decile. The percentage of activities of each section of the check list in each decile according to each criterion was computed. Table XVII shows the percentage of activities of each section in each decile according to frequency of performance; Table XVIII shows the same thing according to need for training; and Table XIX shows the same thing according to value to the student teacher.

In studying Tables XVII, XVIII, and XIX, one must keep in mind the number of activities in each section of the check list and in the check list as a whole. These facts are as follows:

SECTION	NUMBER OF ACTIVITIES
I	70
II	70
III	138
IV	75
V	35
VI	32
Total Check List	422

The number of activities of each section of the check list in the tenth decile rank is as follows: Section I (activities relating to children), 6; Section II (activities relating to student teacher), 4; Section III (activities relating to teaching), 31; Section IV (activities relating to school and classroom management), 0; Section V (activities relating to administration of student teaching program), 1; Section VI (miscellaneous activities), 0. This gives a total of 42 activities in the highest decile rank, which is 10 per cent of the total number of activities in the whole check list.

Since the total number of activities of each section of the check list varies, the number of activities of each section in each decile rank can be studied comparatively more easily if reduced to percentages. Only percentages are shown in Tables XVII, XVIII, and XIX.

[3] For decile ranks of each activity according to each criterion see Appendix C.

Examination of Tables XVII, XVIII, and XIX shows that in all three a larger percentage of the activities of the third section (activities relating to teaching) of the check list are in the upper 5 deciles than of any other section. Table XX, compiled from Tables XVII, XVIII, and XIX, shows the percentage of activities of each section of the check list in the upper 5 decile ranks

TABLE XVII

PERCENTAGE OF ACTIVITIES OF EACH SECTION IN EACH DECILE RANK ACCORDING TO FREQUENCY OF PERFORMANCE

DECILE RANK	SECT. I	SECT. II	SECT. III	SECT. IV	SECT. V	SECT. VI
10	8.6	5.7	22.4	0.0	2.9	0.0
9	10.0	2.9	16.7	6.5	17.1	6.3
8	8.6	5.7	21.7	2.6	0.0	3.1
7	7.1	10.0	11.6	5.2	11.4	12.5
6	5.7	12.9	9.4	11.7	14.3	6.3
5	4.3	17.1	5.1	20.8	0.0	12.5
4	12.9	8.6	5.8	10.4	5.7	25.0
3	21.4	15.7	3.6	11.7	8.6	0.0
2	11.4	14.3	2.9	12.9	22.8	9.4
1	10.0	7.1	0.7	18.2	17.1	25.0

Note: The table reads: 8.6 per cent of the 70 activities of Section I of the check list are in the highest decile rank according to frequency of performance; 10.0 per cent are in the ninth decile rank, and so on.

TABLE XVIII

PERCENTAGE OF ACTIVITIES OF EACH SECTION IN EACH DECILE RANK ACCORDING TO NEED FOR TRAINING

DECILE RANK	SECT. I	SECT. II	SECT. III	SECT. IV	SECT. V	SECT. VI
10	27.1	11.4	10.2	0.0	0.0	0.0
9	5.7	17.1	20.3	0.0	0.0	0.0
8	14.3	7.1	25.4	0.0	0.0	0.0
7	11.4	14.3	15.2	2.6	2.9	0.0
6	10.0	14.3	5.8	11.7	14.3	0.0
5	12.9	11.4	7.9	6.5	11.4	9.4
4	4.3	12.9	11.6	6.5	14.3	18.7
3	8.6	1.4	1.4	16.9	11.4	28.1
2	5.7	10.0	2.2	25.9	25.7	25.0
1	0.0	0.0	0.0	29.9	20.0	18.7

Note: The table reads: 27.1 per cent of the 70 activities of Section I of the check list are in the highest decile rank according to need for training; 5.7 per cent are in the ninth decile rank, and so on.

TABLE XIX

PERCENTAGE OF ACTIVITIES OF EACH SECTION IN EACH DECILE RANK ACCORDING TO VALUE TO STUDENT TEACHER

DECILE RANK	SECT. I	SECT. II	SECT. III	SECT. IV	SECT. V	SECT. VI
10	7.1	4.3	25.4	0.0	0.0	0.0
9	11.4	8.6	18.1	3.9	0.0	3.1
8	5.7	4.3	21.0	3.9	2.9	9.3
7	12.9	10.0	8.7	7.8	14.3	6.3
6	15.7	12.9	6.5	2.6	20.0	12.5
5	12.9	8.6	6.5	12.9	14.3	6.3
4	8.6	20.0	3.6	7.8	20.0	12.5
3	12.9	12.9	4.3	12.9	11.4	15.6
2	8.6	2.8	4.3	24.7	11.4	15.6
I	4.3	15.7	1.5	23.4	5.7	18.7

Note: The table reads: 7.1 per cent of the 70 activities of Section I of the check list are in the highest decile rank, according to value to student teacher; 11.4 per cent are in the ninth decile rank, and so on.

according to each criterion. This table shows clearly that supervisors of student teaching, from the standpoint of all three criteria, look upon the teaching as the most important thing with which they are to deal. More than 75 per cent of the activities of the third section (activities relating to teaching) are in the upper 5 decile ranks according to all three criteria. Table XVIII shows that none of the activities of the fourth section (activities relating to school and classroom management) and none of the activities of the fifth section (activities relating to administration of the student teaching program) are in the upper 3 decile ranks, when

TABLE XX

PERCENTAGE OF ACTIVITIES OF EACH SECTION IN THE UPPER FIVE DECILES ACCORDING TO EACH CRITERION

CRITERIA	SECT. I	SECT. II	SECT. III	SECT. IV	SECT. V	SECT. VI
Frequency of Performance	40.0	37.2	81.8	26.0	45.7	28.2
Need for Training .	68.5	64.2	76.9	14.3	17.2	0.0
Value to Student Teacher	52.8	40.1	79.7	18.2	37.2	31.2

Note: The table reads: 40.0 per cent of the activities of Section I of the check list are in the upper five decile ranks according to frequency of performance; 68.5 per cent are in the upper five decile ranks according to need for training; and so on.

the criterion of *need for training* is considered. None of the activities of the sixth section (a group of miscellaneous supervisory activities) is in the upper 5 decile ranks when *need for training* is considered.

RATING OF ACTIVITIES FOR FREQUENCY OF PERFORMANCE

It is significant that every one of the 422 activities of the check list is performed by some supervisors. Only 14, however, are "100 per cent" activities, *i.e.*, activities performed by all the training supervisors. None of these 14 activities was given a rating of 4 in Column 1 of the check list.[4] Of these 14 activities, 2 relate to children, and 12 relate to teaching. These "100 per cent" activities are as follows:

Protect pupils from inaccuracies of student teacher   (I-3)[5]
Give advice concerning disciplinary problems   (I-54)
Discuss lesson aims   (III-3)
Consider experiences of children in planning lessons   (III-4)
Consider needs of children in planning lessons   (III-5)
Consider abilities of children in planning lessons   (III-7)
Get all supplementary teaching materials ready before starting to teach the lesson   (III-26)
Observe teaching of student   (III-33)
Discuss procedure with student   (III-36)
Teach place of pupil-activity in lesson   (III-37)
Teach how to secure attention   (III-93)
Hold student teacher responsible for securing attention   (III-94)
Teach student teacher to see the poor points in his teaching   (III-96)
Teach student teacher to see why the poor points in his teaching are poor   (III-97)

Study of these "100 per cent" activities reveals that all the supervisors are fairly cognizant of their responsibilities as far as teaching the children and training the student teacher to teach the children are concerned, if teaching is thought of in a limited sense. Discipline, lesson planning, consideration of the needs and abilities of the children, seeing that all supplementary materials

---

[4] The reader is referred at this point to the statement of instructions relating to rating the activities from the standpoint of frequency. A little later we shall speak of activities which are frequently performed by different groups of supervisors. Such activities were given a rating of 1 in Column 1 of the check list by the supervisors making up such groups.

[5] The numbers within the parentheses refer to section and activity numbers of the check list. This particular activity is the third activity in the first section. For complete statement of the activity see Appendix A, p. 80.

are ready before starting to teach, observation of the student's teaching, discussion of his teaching procedure with student, place of pupil-activity in the lesson, problem of attention, and analysis of poor points in student's teaching constitute the "100 per cent" list of supervisory activities.

It is interesting to compare the "100 per cent" list of activities with the list of activities *performed frequently* by 90 per cent or more of the supervisors. This is a list of 11 activities, 1 being in Section I (activities relating to children), 9 in Section III (activities relating to teaching), and 1 in Section V (activities relating to administration of the student teaching program). The activities making up this list are as follows:

Give advice concerning disciplinary problems   (I-54)
Discuss lesson aims   (III-3)
Consider needs of children in planning lessons   (III-5)
Consider interests of children in planning lessons   (III-6)
Consider abilities of children in planning lessons   (III-7)
Correct student teacher's lesson plan   (III-16)
Show that lesson planning is essential to good teaching   (III-25)
Get all supplementary teaching materials ready before starting to teach lesson   (III-26)
Observe teaching of student   (III-33)
Hold student teacher responsible for securing attention   (III-94)
Grade teaching of student teacher at the end of the term   (V-16)

Comparison of the two lists shows that only 7 activities found in the "100 per cent" list are also found in the "90 per cent" list. Certain activities which one would expect to find in the "90 per cent" list are not there. For example, the activity of requiring the student to hold the attention of the children when he teaches is in the "90 per cent" list, while the one of teaching the student how to hold the attention is not. Surely student teachers wish to hold the attention of their pupils when they teach and will do so if they know how and can. The remaining 7 activities of the "100 per cent" list not found in the "90 per cent" list of frequently performed activities are: protect pupils from inaccuracies of student teacher, consider experiences of children in planning lessons, discuss his teaching procedure with pupil, teach place of pupil-activity in the lesson, teach how to secure attention, teach student to see the poor points in his teaching, and teach student to see why the poor points in his teaching are poor.

A list of activities *performed frequently* by from 80 to 90 per cent of the supervisors was also prepared. The activities in the "80 per cent" list are as follows:

Bear responsibility for progress of children (I-2)
See that pupils do not suffer from inaccuracies of student teacher (I-3)
See that children are happy in the classroom (I-55)
Teach student teacher how to make children happy in the classroom (I-56)
Create proper attitude toward children (II-1)
Create proper attitude toward student teaching (II-2)
Teach student teacher to analyze himself as a prospective teacher (II-3)
Confer with student teacher wishing to help in the preparation of his lesson (II-36)
Tell student teacher of valuable references (II-49)
Consider experiences of children in planning lessons (III-4)
Consider abilities of children in planning lessons (III-7)
Use pupil experiences appropriate for lessons to be taught (III-9)
Use experiences from everyday life to vitalize subject matter of lesson (III-10)
See that lesson provides for pupil motive (III-11)
Discuss lesson plan with student teacher (III-18)
Provide natural teaching situation for student's first lessons (III-19)
Help student plan units of work (III-20)
Show student what preparation for teaching a lesson involves (III-27)
Teach demonstration lessons for student teacher (III-28)
Analyze student's teaching procedure carefully before conferring with him (III-34)
Discuss procedure with student (III-36)
Teach place of pupil-activity in the lesson (III-37)
Teach place of subject matter in the lesson (III-38)
Train student teacher to carry on drill work (III-75)
Teach how to secure attention (III-93)
Teach student teacher to see the good points in his lesson (III-95)
Teach student teacher to see the poor points in his lesson (III-96)
Teach student teacher to see why the poor points in his teaching are poor (III-97)
Teach student teacher to see why the good points in his teaching are good (III-98)
Train student teacher to hold children responsible for accuracy of facts (III-99)
Hold student teacher responsible for progress of children when he teaches (III-100)
Teach student teacher to test progress of children (III-101)
Hold student teacher responsible for meeting and dismissing classes on time (IV-63)
Note problems which occur in student teaching (V-2)

Report at end of term a detailed statement of student teacher's fitness to teach (V-15)

Report term grade of student teacher to director of training (V-17)

The 7 activities of the "100 per cent" list which did not appear in the "90 per cent" list appear in this "80 per cent" list of activities. The 14 rather formal activities of the "100 per cent" list are performed frequently by 80 per cent and more of the supervisors. There would be, perhaps, no criticism of supervisors for performing these particular activities if the list were larger and if the modern tendencies of education were more generously represented. The list of 11 activities performed frequently by 90 per cent of the supervisors contains no mention of an activity which is any better than the "100 per cent" list, with the possible exception of the one dealing with interests of children. The "90 per cent" list does not contain the activity dealing with the place of pupil-activity in the lesson, which is in the "100 per cent" list.

On the other hand, a few activities in harmony with tendencies in modern education do appear in the list of activities reported as being performed frequently by 80 to 90 per cent of the supervisors. Making children happy in the classroom, using pupil experiences as bases for lessons, using experiences of everyday life to vitalize subject matter of lesson, and diagnostic testing of progress of children appear in the "80 per cent" list. It is a striking fact, however, that such activities as directing student teacher to study interests of children, respecting personality of the child, making student teacher feel at home in the classroom, respecting opinions of student teacher, having such relation to student teacher that he is at his best when with the supervisor, teaching student teacher how to select and to organize subject matter, giving student teacher responsibility for teaching a complete unit of subject matter, teaching student teacher to apply psychological principles with respect to individual differences, teaching the student teacher to observe the laws of learning in his teaching and visiting homes of children with student teacher are not in any one of these three lists of activities.

The study of the activities not performed by supervisors gives an interesting picture. Only one activity out of the entire number making up the check list is not performed at all by as many as 90 per cent of the supervisors. This activity is: Teach student teacher to supervise washing of windows by children (IV-40).[6] It is not performed at all by 326 supervisors. Four activities are not performed at all by from 80 to 90 per cent of the supervisors. These four activities are:

> Visit homes of children with student teacher (I-70)
> Require student teacher to report inspections (of toilets, desks, lockers, wardrobes) in writing (IV-33)
> Direct student teacher to wash windows (IV-39)
> Train student teacher to supplement children's lunch with a hot dish (IV-70)

Four activities are not performed at all by from 70 to 80 per cent of the supervisors. These activities are:

> Entertain student teacher at supervisor's home (II-70)
> Give opportunity to observe the meetings of the school council (IV-74)
> Select student teacher's best lesson plan for filing with director of training (V-20)
> Visit classes taught by members of college faculty (V-34)

Twenty-five activities are not performed at all by from 55 to 70 per cent of the supervisors. These activities are:

> Direct student teacher in giving intelligence tests (I-17)
> Supervise tabulating of results of intelligence tests (I-19)
> Inspect children for evidences of diseased tonsils (I-36)
> Inspect children for evidences of adenoids (I-37)
> Require student teacher to hand in notes on readings (II-51)
> Grade student teacher's notes on readings (II-52)
> Entertain student teacher at places other than supervisor's home (II-70)
> Train children in use of card catalog (III-116)
> Inspect toilets (IV-29)
> Inspect children's lockers (IV-32)
> Supervise washing of blackboard by children (IV-41)
> Supervise cleaning of erasers by children (IV-42)
> Give student teacher practice in handling office records (IV-57)
> Give opportunity to participate in parent-teachers' association (IV-68)
> Give opportunity to assist with school teas for parents (IV-69)
> Report term grade of student to registrar (V-18)
> Confer with members of college faculty as to most helpful prerequisite courses for student teacher (V-26)
> Confer with members of college faculty with regard to their courses (V-35)

[6] The numbers in parentheses refer to section and activity number of the check list. See Appendix A, p. 88.

Advise with student teacher as to joining National Education Association (VI-8)

Advise with student teacher as to attending National Education Association (VI-9)

Advise with student teacher as to joining district educational association (VI-12)

Advise with student teacher as to attending district educational association (VI-13)

Advise with student teacher as to trips he should take during vacations (VI-22)

Advise with student teacher as to how to benefit from trips taken during vacation (VI-23)

Write bulletins for student teacher on teaching the various subjects (VI-30)

These lists of activities which are not performed at all by large numbers of the supervisors show that many student teachers are failing to have many experiences which they should be having. Further reference will be made to this point later. The lists also show that many supervisors are trying to eliminate many comparatively ineffective activities. Examples of such activities are: washing windows, washing blackboards, and writing bulletins for student teachers on the teaching of various subjects.

Rating of Activities for Need for Training

Examination of the rating of the activities from the standpoint of need for training shows that there is not a single activity in which at least 90 per cent of the supervisors wish they might have had training before undertaking the supervision of student teaching. Only 3 activities were reported by 80 per cent of the training supervisors as ones in which they wish they might have had training. These three activities are:

Direct student teacher in giving intelligence tests (I-17)
Teach lesson planning (III-1)
Teach student teacher to apply psychological principles with respect to individual differences (III-56)

Seventeen activities are reported by from 70 to 80 per cent of the supervisors as ones in which they wish they might have had training. These are:

Study habits of children (I-5)
Study children as individuals (I-8)
Study mental characteristics of children (I-9)

Classify mental characteristics of children   (I-10)
Study interests of children   (I-13)
Study social attitudes of children   (I-15)
Supervise scoring intelligence tests   (I-18)
Supervise tabulating results of intelligence tests   (I-19)
Make usable records of intelligence tests results   (I-20)
Make use of intelligence scores in planning work   (I-21)
Give achievement tests to children   (I-22)
Help student teacher develop a good teaching voice   (II-19)
Show student teacher relation of lesson plans to larger objectives of the school   (III-2)
Teach student teacher to interpret what is observed in terms of the laws of learning   (III-30)
Teach student teacher how to select subject matter   (III-47)
Teach student teacher how to organize subject matter   (III-48)
Help student teacher to build up a teaching technique based on psychological principles   (III-136)

Twenty-eight activities are reported by from 60 to 70 per cent of the supervisors as ones in which they wish they might have had training. These are:

Classify habits of children   (I-6)
Study children as a group   (I-7)
Study personal characteristics of children   (I-11)
Classify interests of children   (I-14)
Classify social attitudes of children   (I-16)
Supervise scoring achievement tests   (I-23)
Supervise tabulating results of achievement tests   (I-24)
Make usable records of achievement tests results   (I-25)
Make use of achievement tests scores in planning work   (I-26)
Direct student teacher to analyze his writing from standpoint of system being taught children   (II-5)
Teach student teacher to be attentive to his own oral English   (II-6)
Train student teacher in habit of correcting his own oral English   (II-8)
Train student teacher in habit of correcting his own written English   (II-9)
Teach student teacher to study objectively his own achievement in school subjects   (II-10)
Teach student teacher how to study   (II-13)
Direct study of qualities making up best teaching personality   (II-14)
Advise with student teacher with respect to poise of mind when standing before a class   (II-17)
Advise with student teacher as to poise of body when standing before a class   (II-18)
Train student teacher in ways of conserving his vitality   (II-20)
Stimulate and encourage student teacher   (II-21)

Consider experiences of children in planning lessons (III-4)
Consider needs of children in planning lessons (III-5)
Consider interests of children in planning lessons (III-6)
Consider abilities of children in planning lessons (III-7)
Demonstration teaching for student teacher (III-28)
Use standardized tests in connection with teaching (III-41)
Show student teacher time and place for project work (III-70)
Observe laws of learning in teaching (III-87)

An outline presentation of these 48 activities shows more clearly the things in which 60 per cent and more of the supervisors wish they might have had training. Such an outline is as follows:

I. Study of Children
    1. Interests, habits, social attitudes, and mental characteristics
    2. Use of psychological principles in problems of individual differences

II. Study of Subject Matter
    1. Selection and organization of subject matter
    2. Experiences of children as a basis for lesson planning
    3. Lesson planning to meet the interests, needs, and abilities of the children
    4. Relation of lesson planning to the larger objectives of the school

III. Study of Teaching
    1. Demonstration teaching for student teacher
    2. Observation of teaching from standpoint of laws of learning
    3. Building up a teaching technique based upon psychological principles
    4. Project teaching

IV. Use of Tests
    1. Intelligence tests
    2. Achievement tests
    3. Diagnostic testing

V. Study of Student Teacher as a Prospective Teacher
    1. Qualities of good teaching personality
        a. How develop a good teaching voice
        b. How develop bodily and mental poise
        c. How conserve vitality
    2. Study of teacher's achievement in the school subjects
        a. Habits of oral and written English
        b. Penmanship habit
    3. Ability to study
        a. How teach how to study

This outline shows that the activities in which at least 60 per cent of the supervisors wish they might have had training prior to undertaking supervision of student teaching relate to the study of children, subject matter, the use of objective tests, and the student teacher as a prospective teacher.

RATING OF ACTIVITIES FOR VALUE TO THE STUDENT TEACHER

Six activities failed to receive from any of the supervisors the *less than average value* check in Column 3 of the check list. This is evidence that all the supervisors regarded these activities as being either of *better than average value* or of *average value* in the training of student teachers. These 6 activities are:

Study children as individuals (I-8)
Discuss lesson aims with student teacher (III-3)
Consider experiences of children in planning lessons (III-4)
Consider needs of children in planning lessons (III-5)
Consider abilities of children in planning lessons (III-7)
Teach student teacher to determine what parts of lesson are fundamental (III-51)

Twenty activities were reported by 90 per cent of the supervisors as being of *better than average value* in the training of the student teachers. These activities are:

Study children as individuals (I-8)
Give advice concerning disciplinary problems (I-54)
See that student teacher learns that children must be happy in schoolroom (I-55)
Train student teacher in habit of correcting his own written English (II-8)
Discuss lesson aims with student teacher (III-3)
Consider experiences of children in planning lessons (III-4)
Consider needs of children in planning lessons (III-5)
Consider interests of children in planning lessons (III-6)
Consider abilities of children in planning lessons (III-7)
Gather experiences from everyday life to vitalize subject matter of lesson (III-10)
See that lesson provides for pupil motive (III-11)
Help student teacher in planning units of work (III-20)
Show student teacher that planning is essential to good teaching (III-25)
Get all supplementary teaching materials ready before starting to teach the lesson (III-26)
Show student teacher what preparation for teaching involves (III-27)

Teach student teacher the place of pupil-activity in the lesson   (III-37)

Teach student teacher how to secure attention of children when he teaches   (III-93)

Hold student teacher responsible for securing attention of children when he teaches   (III-94)

Teach student teacher to see the poor points in his teaching   (III-96)

Teach the student teacher to see why the poor points in his teaching are poor   (III-97)

Fifty-one activities were reported by from 80 to 90 per cent of the supervisors as being of *better than average value* in the training of the student teacher. These activities are:

Create in children proper attitude toward student teacher   (I-1)

Bear responsibility for progress of children   (I-2)

Study habits of children   (I-5)

Study mental characteristics of children   (I-9)

Study interests of children   (I-13)

Teach student teacher how to respect personality of child   (I-52)

Require student teacher to handle disciplinary problems when he teaches   (I-53)

Teach student teacher how to make children happy in schoolroom (I-56)

Create in student teacher proper attitude toward children   (II-1)

Train student teacher in habit of correcting his own written English (II-9)

Teach student teacher how to study   (II-13)

Tell student teacher of valuable references   (II-49)

Teach lesson planning   (III-1)

Show relation of lesson plans to larger objectives of the school   (III-2)

Discover pupil experiences appropriate for lesson to be taught   (III-8)

Use pupil experiences appropriate for lesson to be taught   (III-9)

Correct student teacher's lesson plan   (III-16)

Discuss corrections made in plan with student teacher   (III-18)

Provide a natural teaching situation for student teacher's first lessons (III-19)

Plan work for the student teacher to organize and work out for himself   (III-21)

Test everything planned from standpoint of children's needs   (III-22)

Test everything planned from standpoint of children's interests (III-23)

Test everything planned from standpoint of children's abilities   (III-24)

Teach demonstration lessons for student teacher   (III-29)

Interpret what is observed in terms of laws of learning   (III-30)

Observe student teacher when he teaches   (III-33)

After observing student teacher, analyze his teaching procedure before conferring with him   (III-34)

Discuss teaching procedure with student teacher   (III-36)

Teach student teacher the place of subject matter in the lesson   (III-38)

Teach student teacher to test his teaching   (III-40)

Direct student teacher to do the necessary "follow-up" teaching with children   (III-43)

Keep before student teacher the thought that subject matter is a means and not an end   (III-46)

Teach student teacher how to select subject matter   (III-47)

Teach student teacher how to organize subject matter   (III-48)

Teach student teacher to determine what parts of lesson are fundamental   (III-51)

Teach student teacher to apply psychological principles with respect to individual differences   (III-56)

Show student teacher time and place for drill work   (III-66)

Direct student teacher to study his own questioning   (III-84)

Observe the laws of learning in teaching   (III-87)

Teach student teacher to see the good points in his teaching   (III-95)

Teach student teacher to see why the good points in his teaching are good   (III-98)

Hold children responsible for accuracy of facts   (III-99)

Hold student teacher responsible for progress of children when he teaches   (III-100)

Test progress of children   (III-101)

Teach correlation of different school subjects   (III-128)

Direct student teacher to sources of good teaching materials   (III-130)

Build up a teaching technique based upon psychological principles   (III-136)

Start collecting good teaching materials   (III-137)

Care for lighting of classroom   (IV-1)

Care for ventilation of classroom   (IV-2)

Supervisor constantly puts herself into place of student teacher   (VI-32)

These activities cover thoroughly the task of classroom instruction.

Here is a total of 33 activities which are not performed at all by from 55 to 90 per cent of the supervisors; a total of 48 activities in which from 60 to 80 per cent of the supervisors wish they might have had training before they undertook the supervision of student teaching; and a total of 71 activities which are rated as being of *better than average value* in the training of student teachers by from 80 to 90 per cent of the supervisors. One activity, direct student teacher in giving intelligence tests (I-17), is in all three lists. It is interesting to note that Charters and Waples[7]

[7] Charters, W. W. and Waples, Douglas, *The Commonwealth Teacher-Training Study*, p. 513. University of Chicago Press, 1929. The attention of the reader is called to the fact that Charters and Waples number the deciles from 1 to 10, 1 being the highest and 10 the lowest decile. In comparisons with this study the deciles of Charters and Waples have been renumbered in accordance with standard statistical procedure.

report that intermediate grade teachers rate the activity, giving intelligence tests, in the seventh decile from the standpoint of *importance* and in the ninth decile from the standpoint of *desirability of preservice training*; and that primary grade teachers rate the same activity in the tenth decile from the standpoint both of *importance* and of *desirability of preservice training*.

Four activities[8] of the check list relate to the parents and the home life of the children. These four activities and their respective decile ranks are as follows :[9]

	F	N	V
Study home life of children	3	6	4
Keep in touch with parents of children	2	3	3
Keep parents informed of progress of children	3	3	4
Visit homes of children	1	2	1

Charters and Waples report that intermediate grade teachers rate the activity, Obtaining advice and information from parents, in the ninth decile for *importance* and in the eighth decile for *desirability of preservice training*; and that primary grade teachers rate the same activity in the ninth decile for *importance* and in the seventh decile for *desirability of preservice training*.[10]

The decile ranks of the items of the check list show further that student teachers are having little or no opportunity to learn how to take care of the health needs of pupils. Charters and Waples report that both intermediate and primary grade teachers rate the various activities which relate to the health needs of the children in no case lower than the seventh decile for *importance* and *desirability of preservice training*.[11] They report that many of the activities relating to health are in the tenth decile for both *importance* and *desirability of preservice training* in the judgment of experienced intermediate and primary grade teachers.

According to the rating of the activities of the check list by training supervisors, student teachers are having little or no opportunity to direct extra-class activities. Section IV (activities relating to school and classroom management) has 15 activities

[8] See Activities 61, 62, 63, and 70 of Section I of the check list, Appendix A, p. 80.

[9] Under F are indicated the decile ranks for *frequency of performance*; under N are indicated the decile ranks for *need for training*; and under V are indicated the decile ranks for *value to the student teacher*.

[10] Charters and Waples, *op. cit.*, p. 513.

[11] Charters and Waples, *op. cit.*, pp. 502–513.

relating to extra-class work, such as programs for special days and special weeks, school parties, school programs, parent-teachers' association, and school teas for parents. These activities are in the fifth decile rank or lower for all three criteria. Charters and Waples report a rather long list of activities relating to extra-class work. Those corresponding most nearly to the activities listed above tend to fall in the upper four decile ranks for *desirability of preservice training* in the judgment of experienced intermediate and primary grade teachers.[12]

It is evident that many of the activities rated by the supervisors as being in the fifth decile rank or lower are really significant. Many of the supervisors were conscious of this when filling out the check list for they often wrote on the margin a statement to the effect that the activity was of value but that the time spent by the student teacher in the training school was so short that the activity could not be performed.

Influence of Training and Experience upon Significant Activities

Thirty-eight selected activities were studied with a view to seeing just what differences there were in the ratings made by groups of supervisors differing in training and experience. The thirty-eight activities so studied are:

> Use achievement test scores in planning work   (I-26)
> Inspect children for evidences of nervousness   (I-42)
> Give special attention to children who stutter and stammer   (I-43)
> Show the necessity of respecting personality of child   (I-51)
> Teach how to respect personality of child   (I-52)
> Study home life of children   (I-61)
> Keep in touch with parents of children   (I-62)
> Keep parents informed of progress of children   (I-63)
> Make student teacher feel at home in classroom   (II-31)
> Respect opinions of student teacher   (II-32)
> Have such relation to student teacher that he is always at his best when with supervisor   (II-33)
> Keep a record of student teacher's progress   (II-57)
> Keep a record of student teacher's needs   (II-58)
> Watch for original or creative work by children   (III-12)
> Keep records of original or creative work by children   (III-13)
> Discover factors influencing child to do original work   (III-14)

[12] Charters and Waples, *op. cit.*, pp. 520–522.

Plan work for the student to organize and work out for himself (III-21)

Interpret what is observed in terms of laws of learning (III-30)

Use standardized tests in connection with teaching (III-41)

Use informal objective tests in connection with teaching (III-42)

Give student teacher responsibility for selecting and organizing a complete unit of subject matter (III-49)

Give student teacher responsibility for teaching a complete unit of subject matter (III-50)

Show time and place for construction work as a means of expression of ideas (III-72)

Show time and place for creative work (III-73)

Show time and place for appreciation lesson (III-74)

Study examples of thinking on part of children (III-85)

Make diagnostic records of the work of each pupil (III-102)

Use diagnostic records of pupils in teaching (III-103)

Teach pupils to make their own diagnostic records (III-104)

Use community life as a source for teaching materials (III-110)

Plan school excursions (III-131)

Visit institutions and places of business to make arrangements for school excursions (III-132)

Teach student teacher to carry out plans for school excursions (III-133)

Teach principles guiding proper placement of school furniture (IV-7)

Teach principles for caring for physical conditions of classroom (IV-8)

Teach supervision of children at indoor play (IV-43)

Teach supervision of children at play on playground (IV-44)

Give opportunity to participate in parent-teachers' association (IV-68)

The activities listed above were selected because it was thought that they represent fairly well some of the modern tendencies in education.

The three groups of supervisors, whose ratings of these selected activities were studied, are spoken of as Groups A, B, and C. The training and experience of these three groups are shown in Table XXI. Every member of Group C holds the master's degree and no member of either Group A or B holds any degree. It was desired to have one group of supervisors of limited training and of limited experience, a second group of limited training but of considerable experience, and a third group of considerable training and of considerable experience.

What may be called a *frequency of performance* score, a *need for training* score, and a *value to the student teacher* score were determined for each activity from the corresponding composite

TABLE XXI

Training and Experience of Three Groups of Supervisors Whose Ratings of Significant Activities Were Studied

Group	Number in Group	Median Length of Training	Median Total Teaching Experience	Median Supervisory Experience
A	23	3.9 years	3.7 years	0.7 years
B	21	2.7 years	27.3 years	18.0 years
C	30	5.8 years	13.4 years	5.0 years

ratings by each of the three groups of supervisors.[13] The median score for the group of selected activities for each criterion is shown in Table XXII. Since a rating of 1 for *frequency of performance* is the highest rating based on that criterion, the nearer the median score is to 1, the higher it is. The same is true of median scores shown in Table XXII. Since a rating of 1 for *frequency of performance* is the highest rating based on that cri-

TABLE XXII

Showing Median Scores, and Variability and Percentage of Variability of Median Scores, for Selected Activities by Groups of Supervisors of Different Training and Experience

Group	Frequency of Performance			Need for Training			Value to Student Teacher		
	Med.	Q	Per Cent of Variability	Med.	Q	Per Cent of Variability	Med.	Q	Per Cent of Variability
A	2.00	0.49	24.5	36.1	11.2	31.0	1.43	0.18	12.6
B	1.80	0.41	22.6	38.3	13.2	34.4	1.32	0.17	12.8
C	1.93	0.47	24.4	50.0	11.2	22.4	1.48	0.14	9.5

Note: The table reads: The median score for the selected activities as determined from the ratings by the supervisors of Group A is 2.00, Q is 0.49, and the per cent of variability is 24.5 when the criterion of *frequency of performance* is considered, etc.

[13] The method of computing the composite ratings of an activity for each group is described in the footnote on page 30. The *frequency of performance* score for an activity was found by dividing the corresponding composite rating by the number of supervisors whose individual ratings are represented in the composite rating. The *value to the student teacher* score is similarly found. The *need for training* score is merely the percentage of the group indicating need for training in any particular activity.

terion, the nearer the median score is to 1, the higher it is. The same is true of median scores based on the criterion of *value to student teacher*. These two facts must be remembered in interpreting Table XXII.

Examination of the table does not show that the scores made by Group C, which was made up of well-trained and experienced supervisors, are markedly different from those made by Group A, which was made up of inexperienced supervisors of limited training, or from those made by Group B, which was made up of experienced supervisors of limited training. One or two tendencies are evident, however. The *need for training* score made by Group C is considerably larger than that made by either of the other two groups. The variability is considerably smaller, too. There is greater unity of agreement in Group C with respect to what is of value to the student teacher than there is in the case of the other two groups, although the median score by Group C based on this criterion is the lowest one.

The table suggests that a mere checking of a list of supervisory activities from the standpoint of *frequency of performance* and *value to the student teacher* by a group of supervisors, made up of individual supervisors differing in merit, would show no marked differences. The real differences between the poor and excellent supervisors are revealed in the procedures or techniques used in carrying on these activities. That these differences are revealed in the actual work of such supervisors is apparent after a study is made of the reports by student teachers of their experiences in student teaching. So far as this study is concerned no further data bearing on this problem have been gathered.

Summary

Analysis of the supervisory activities performed by training supervisors in carrying on their work with student teachers has disclosed many interesting facts, such as the following:

1. The analysis reveals a marked tendency on the part of supervisors to limit the experiences of the student teacher to classroom instruction. Even classroom instruction tends to be done in piecemeal fashion, so far as many student teachers are concerned, for only 60 per cent of the supervisors frequently give the student teacher responsibility for organizing and teaching a complete unit of subject matter. In connection with this fact it must be remem-

bered that more than 60 per cent of the supervisors whose activities are reported in this study work in affiliated public schools. Public school teachers very likely enjoy teaching too well themselves and they feel that the work is too important to intrust too much of it to a novice. They perhaps fail to see that the very importance of teaching is the reason the novice is there with them and that their responsibility, because of its importance, is to induct the novice into all the teacher's work.

The supervisors rank below the sixth decile 75 per cent of the activities of Section IV (activities relating to school and classroom management) for *frequency of performance*, 85 per cent for *need for training*, and 82 per cent for *value to student teacher*. This does not seem to give much support to writers of manuals of observation, participation, and student teaching who devote to problems of school and classroom management so much space in their manuals.

2. A study of the activities in which supervisors wish they might have had training before undertaking the supervision of student teaching shows that supervisors do have a wider vision of their work than the activities which they perform indicate. They want to study children, their interests, habits, social attitudes, and mental characteristics. They want this study of children placed upon a psychological basis so that they may come to see the underlying psychological principles which will enable a teacher to understand child life and its development. They want to study the problem of the selection and organization of subject matter, and the experiences of children as a basis for lesson planning; they want to study lesson planning in the light of the interests, needs, and abilities of children and to see the relation of lesson planning to the larger objectives of the school. Supervisors of student teaching want to study teaching in the concrete and in the light of the laws of learning, in order to evolve a concept of teaching technique which is based upon psychological principles. They want training in giving and scoring standardized tests so that they may carry on a program of diagnostic testing. Finally, they want to study the student teacher as a prospective teacher so that they may efficiently aid him in realizing his potentialities.

Directors of training will be able to obtain from these suggestions by supervisors in service the basis for a training program for prospective supervisors.

3. A study of the activities to which supervisors give a high rating for value to the student teacher shows that supervisors feel that the student teacher should recognize that he is preparing himself to teach children. This is evidenced by the fact that at least 80 per cent of supervisors rate, as being of better than average value to the student teacher, such activities as follows: respect personality of child; discover and use pupil experiences appropriate for lesson to be taught; test everything planned from standpoint of needs, interests, and abilities of children; study teaching in terms of the laws of learning; and keep uppermost the thought that subject matter is a means and not an end.

On the other hand, the training supervisors tend to see for the student teacher little value in activities relating to the study of the home life of the pupils, activities relating to extra-class work, and activities relating to intelligence testing.

Executives in teacher training institutions who are expanding their training facilities by affiliating with public schools for training purposes must be careful in selecting for supervisory work teachers who will be able to vision clearly what the task of the supervisor of student teachers is.

4. Attempts to discover the influence of training and experience of the individual supervisor upon the ratings given to selected activities availed little. The differences are not marked. The most significant difference found between the ratings given by groups of supervisors varying in experience and training was that a larger percentage of the trained and experienced group sees the need for specific training before undertaking the supervision of student teaching. There tends also to be less variability in the ratings given by the trained and experienced group. It is likely that the real differences in the work of supervisors of different merit lie not so much in the activities which they perform as in the procedures or techniques used in performing these activities. To bring out the evidence in support of this contention is the purpose of the next two chapters of this study.

CHAPTER V

EVALUATION OF SUPERVISORY ACTIVITIES BY STUDENT TEACHERS

Statements evaluating their experiences as student teachers were secured from 411 student teachers in six normal schools and teachers colleges. These statements were given by the student teachers in response to this request:

1. List all things which your critic teachers have done for you, or provided opportunities for you to do, which have helped you.
2. List all things which you wanted your critics to do for you, or to provide opportunities for you to do, which were not done.

The 411 student teachers replying to this request are distributed among the six schools as follows:

School	Number of Student Teachers
A	64
B	112
C	25
D	70
E	74
F	66
Total	411

Three typical statements by student teachers are given in full. The first statement was submitted by a student teacher who had spent one period a day for two terms of twelve weeks each in the training school. The statement follows:

I. Things my critics did for me, or provided opportunities for me to do, which helped me:

    1. My critics have caused me to have an appreciation of and a love for good teaching.

2. I have seen the effects which good teaching has had upon the pupils.

3. I have been able to express my whole self while working under the supervision of my critics.

4. I have learned through their help to know more about the characteristics of the intermediate grade child.

5. I have learned to know better how pupils learn.

6. I have become acquainted with the best practical methods for teaching the subjects I taught.

7. I have started to cultivate better habits of health, promptness, manner, and speech since I have learned how much a teacher is held as an ideal by the pupils.

8. My critics helped me with my lesson plans, thus enabling me to teach more effectively.

9. My critics helped me to analyze their teaching, my teaching, and myself according to psychological principles.

10. My critics helped me to become acquainted with the clerical work of a teacher, and tried to give me experience along every phase of school teaching.

II. Things I wanted my critics to do for me, or to provide opportunities for me to do, which were not done:

1. I was with the pupils such a short time that I did not come really to know the pupils so well as I shall in a schoolroom of my own. I did not feel sure of myself in punishing pupils when I met disciplinary problems. I do not think my critics were to blame for this, however. My critics did all that I expected them to do in way of teaching. I should have liked to have had more conferences so as to talk about problems which I think I shall meet later, such as what to do on the first day of school and during the first week.

This second statement of experiences in student teaching was submitted by a student teacher who had completed twenty-six weeks of work. The statement follows:

I. Things my critic did for me, or provided opportunities for me to do, which helped me:

1. One critic gave me an opportunity for planning seating of pupils in the classroom. She gave me suggestions in this which helped me in meeting individual defects, such as sight and hearing.

2. My critic let me grade papers and determine term grades. Then we compared my grades with hers.

3. One critic gave me a well-selected bibliography of teaching materials and methods.

4. One critic taught lessons from time to time which exemplified something she wished me to use in my teaching.

5. My critics went over each lesson with me after the lesson had been taught and gave constructive criticism.

6. One of my critics talked with me about educational meetings she attended and gave me many new ideas.

7. One critic helped in the health service of the school. I got a little experience in first aid and health inspection work.

8. I was given opportunity to help in giving and scoring tests and in recording test scores.

9. I was helped with my voice. The critic would place a V on the back blackboard. I have no trouble now.

10. I acquired poise of body and of mind as the result of the friendly talks with my critics.

11. I am now able to cope with situations which may arise while I am teaching.

12. I have learned to see the child's point of view.

13. I have also found out that the teacher must command authority.

14. I am able to find those things which will call forth the best interest and effort from a group of children.

15. I have been allowed to express my own ideas. When I taught I had full charge of the class.

16. I have been given fine ideas as to the qualities of the best type of discipline.

17. I have been allowed to teach a whole afternoon and a whole week.

18. I have been allowed to make up and use an informal objective test.

19. I have been treated as an equal and the children have recognized me as such.

II. Things I wanted my critics to do for me, or to provide opportunities for me to do, which were not done:

1. I wish I had been given a general scope of the subject matter to be taught at the first, rather than piece by piece through the term.

2. I should have liked to have had my lesson plan returned with corrections before I taught the lesson.

3. I should have liked to have known the home background of some children before trying to teach them.

4. The duties of a student teacher should be stated, if possible. Some critics like it if a student goes ahead and others do not.

5. While teaching a certain subject it would have helped me to have eliminated some of the very detailed things which I was putting into my plans and to have spent the time preparing my lesson; my plans were frequently seven and eight pages long and very detailed—the old-fashioned type.

6. In teaching one subject more preparation would have helped me. I did not know what the new lesson was until I arrived at the school. I thus had little time for preparation.

7. I should have liked to have had some practical experience in taking care of the register, and other records and reports.

In contrast with these two statements is one other which commends and, at the same time, condemns rather severely the supervisors with whom the student teacher worked. This statement was submitted by a student teacher who had completed sixteen weeks of work in student teaching.[1] The statement is:

I. Things my critics did for me, or provided opportunities for me to do, which helped me:
1. Gave me correct attitude toward children.
2. Gave me constructive criticisms of my work.
3. Held conferences with me at the end of each day's teaching.
4. Gave me independent charge of classwork.
5. Gave me supervisory charge of whole room.
6. Gave me independent charge of recreation.
7. Gave me opportunities for fuller development of initiative and responsibility.
8. Gave me better knowledge of skills.

II. Things done by my critics which did not help me:
1. Reprimanded me in front of pupils.
2. Gave me destructive criticisms without explanation.
3. Gave me few or no helpful suggestions.
4. Showed lack of understanding and coöperation.
5. Showed aloofness.
6. Showed hypocrisy; gave me praise but reported caustic criticism on teaching sheet.
7. Suppressed originality; usually desired and demanded imitation.
8. Frequently had an air of antagonism.
9. Showed inaccuracy of subject matter.
10. Discouraged me.

A summary of the statements relating to their experiences in student teaching by the 411 student teachers is given in Tables XXIII and XXIV. The summary of helpful things performed by supervisors is given in Table XXIII and the summary of the things which student teachers wish they had experienced in student teaching is given in Table XXIV.

In compiling these summary tables from the statements by the student teachers care has been taken to use a sufficient number of class headings to insure that the original meaning of the indi-

[1] See Appendix D for statements of experiences in student teaching by other student teachers.

vidual items will not be lost. A comparison of the three foregoing statements with the summary tables shows, however, that the presence or lack of rich content in the experiences of the student teachers has been obscured somewhat. This fact is cited to support the contention that the essential differences between supervisors differing in merit are revealed not so much in the activities per-

TABLE XXIII

HELPFUL THINGS PERFORMED BY SUPERVISORS AS REPORTED BY 411 STUDENT TEACHERS IN SIX NORMAL SCHOOLS AND TEACHERS COLLEGES

HELPFUL THINGS	SCHOOL						
	A	B	C	D	E	F	Total
Gave constructive criticism relating to teaching process .	60	82	25	50	49	57	323
Gave help with lesson planning (daily, unit)...........	26	59	11	34	40	20	190
Gave suggestions relating to teaching materials	20	78	2	18	21	22	161
Gave suggestions relating to classroom management	28	45	12	7	40	16	140
Gave student full charge of room when teaching	30	36	8	9	45	8	136
Gave suggestions relating to problem of individual differences	31	42	3	11	19	11	117
Gave suggestions relating to discipline	35	45	4	15	14	3	116
Permitted student to try out his own ideas	22	32	2	18	30	7	111
Taught demonstration lessons	29	18	13	6	7	37	110
Gave student helpful bibliography	9	20	2	15	2	49	97
Helped improve student's personality	16	28	3	25	14	2	88
Encouraged and inspired student teacher	9	30	2	20	14	2	77
Gave opportunity for making out term grades and reports	20	29	8	3	16	0	76
Gave suggestions relating to use of informal objective tests	8	25	0	3	0	0	36
Gave student charge of playground	0	0	0	2	30	0	32
Permitted student to select subject matter to be taught .	7	1	2	0	15	2	27
Permitted student to take children on field trip or excursion	2	0	0	3	12	5	22
Helped student correct his oral and written English	9	9	0	4	0	0	22
Gave opportunity to participate in extra-curricular activities	17	0	0	0	0	5	22
Created in children right attitude toward student teacher	0	8	0	0	7	6	21
Gave suggestions for study of children's home life	4	2	0	0	5	3	14
Gave suggestions relating to study of how a child learns .	2	3	1	2	2	3	13
Gave opportunity to show initiative	0	1	0	12	0	0	13
Helped student with his writing (printing)	2	3	1	1	2	3	12
Gave student clear assignments	2	0	3	0	2	5	12
Gave suggestions relating to correlation of school subjects	2	1	0	2	0	6	11
Taught use of mimeograph and lantern and slides	0	10	0	0	0	0	10
Gave opportunity to give and score standardized tests ..	2	1	1	0	1	5	10
Taught to see child's point of view	1	2	1	0	1	1	6
Gave opportunity to attend Parent-Teachers' Association	4	0	0	0	0	0	4
Gave opportunity to participate in health inspection ...	2	2	0	0	0	0	4
Gave suggestions relating to writing letters of application	0	0	0	2	0	0	2
Showed how to secure coöperation of parents	2	0	0	0	0	0	2
Gave opportunity to teach an observation lesson	0	0	0	1	0	0	1

TABLE XXIV

DESIRABLE THINGS WANTED IN STUDENT TEACHING AS REPORTED BY 411
STUDENT TEACHERS IN SIX NORMAL SCHOOLS AND TEACHERS COLLEGES

DESIRABLE THINGS WANTED	SCHOOL						
	A	B	C	D	E	F	Total
More constructive criticism relating to teaching process	14	58	6	25	37	14	154
Full charge of classroom when teaching	7	23	1	2	41	15	89
To teach a larger number of different subjects	11	16	0	17	17	5	66
New teaching procedure demonstrated	13	2	4	9	2	12	42
Opportunity to use own ideas	2	14	1	1	16	2	36
Friendlier attitude on part of critic teacher	2	6	0	0	21	1	30
No interruptions or criticisms while teaching a class	0	6	0	0	15	8	29
Opportunity to make out term grades and reports	7	11	0	2	3	0	23
More opportunity to do real teaching	0	8	0	1	10	1	20
Critic to create proper attitude in pupils toward student teacher	0	6	0	0	12	1	19
Suggestions relating to problem of individual differences.	3	2	0	5	0	8	18
More definite assignments	0	8	0	2	4	1	15
A longer period each day for student teaching	9	3	0	2	0	0	14
Selected bibliography of helpful teaching materials and methods	0	4	7	0	2	1	14
Opportunity to come to know the pupils	0	12	0	0	0	0	12
Suggestions relating to discipline	0	0	0	8	0	1	9
Opportunity to use informal objective and standardized tests	4	4	0	0	1	0	9
Perspective of term's work at the beginning	0	6	0	0	3	0	9
To be encouraged	0	0	0	2	4	2	8
To attend Parent-Teachers' Association	1	0	0	3	4	0	8
Suggestions relating to school management	5	0	1	2	0	0	8
Opportunity to conduct opening exercises	4	1	0	0	3	0	8
More freedom in selecting subject matter to be taught ..	3	0	0	0	0	4	7
Knowledge of progress as a teacher	0	0	0	0	1	6	7
To supervise playground	3	0	0	0	4	0	7
Knowledge of points on rating card	0	7	0	0	0	0	7
Opportunity to try methods learned in normal school ...	0	2	0	0	5	0	7
More help in developing teaching personality	0	6	0	0	0	0	6
Opportunity to participate in extra-curricular activities .	0	1	0	0	5	0	6
Desk space and chair provided for student teacher	0	0	0	0	0	5	5
To see critic teacher's lesson plans	4	0	0	0	0	0	4
Less unnecessary preparation	0	0	0	0	4	0	4
Corrected lesson plans returned early enough to permit making needed changes before class time	0	0	0	0	1	2	3
Opportunity to give first aid	2	0	0	0	0	0	2
More flexible lesson plan form	0	2	0	0	0	0	2
A copy of course of study	1	0	0	1	0	0	2
Opportunity to take pupils on field trip	0	0	0	0	0	1	1
Opportunity to correct pupils' English	0	0	0	0	0	1	1
An informed critic teacher	0	0	0	0	1	0	1
Part of student teaching in rural school	0	0	0	0	1	0	1
Contact with all of a teacher's work	0	1	0	0	0	0	1

formed but rather in the techniques used in carrying on the activities.

Examination of Tables XXIII and XXIV reveals a tendency for student teachers to want more opportunity to do those things or to have those things done which they themselves find most helpful. For example, constructive criticism relating to the teaching process has the greatest frequency in both tables. Of the 411 student teachers, 323 report that supervisors gave them constructive criticism relating to the teaching process while only 13 report that their supervisors gave suggestions relating to study of how a child learns. A question might be raised here as to whether both supervisors and student teachers are looking upon the teaching as the important thing rather than the learning by the child.

The item, full charge of classroom when teaching, is in fifth place in Table XXIII and in second place in Table XXIV. Both in a positive and in a negative way the student teachers indicate that they desire to have full charge when they teach. The item, permitted student teacher to try out his own ideas, is in the eighth place in Table XXIII. Of the 411 student teachers whose statements were reported, 111 bear testimony to the fact that they were permitted to use their own ideas. This is a most hopeful piece of evidence. Working conditions which permit a worker to use his own ideas are necessary if he is to experience challenge of effort and attain maximum growth. Such conditions are also necessary if the theory taught in the normal school or teachers college is going to carry over into the training school. In Table XXIV we find that 36 student teachers wanted the opportunity to use their own ideas and 7 wanted the opportunity to try methods learned in the normal school.

It is interesting to note that only 190 of the 411 student teachers report their work in lesson planning as having been helpful to them. This fact should cause supervisors to study rather carefully the way in which they are conducting this work.

Of the 411 student teachers, only 77 report that their supervisors encouraged and inspired them. Table XXIV shows that 30 student teachers wanted their supervisors to show a friendlier attitude and 8 wanted to be encouraged. These three facts indicate that supervisors are failing to build up the right relationship between themselves and the student teachers.

An examination of all the items reported in Tables XXIII and XXIV by the student teachers in the different schools reveals that the program of student supervision varies considerably from school to school. In Table XXIII take, for example, the item of giving suggestions as to use of informal objective tests. In School A, 8 students report that their supervisors gave them this help; in School B, 25 so report; and in School D only 3 so report. In Schools C, E, and F no students report that their supervisors gave them this help. Statements as to experiences in student teaching were secured from 66 student teachers in School D. The fact that the number of students reporting helpful things performed and desirable things wanted, is small, for the most part, would indicate that a rather serious situation may exist in the training school. The students have little to report that is helpful in their student teaching and they seemingly are satisfied with what they are getting.

SUMMARY

While no attempt has been made to compare the rating of the activities of the check list by the supervisors of one normal school or teachers college with the ratings by the supervisors of another school it would seem that there are real differences in the programs of student teaching which are offered in various schools. Efforts to show that ratings of the activities of the check list by groups of supervisors varying in experience and in training availed little. With a number of selected activities there was little difference between the ratings by the various groups. That there are real differences in programs of student teaching offered in different schools and by supervisors in the same school the facts of this chapter clearly show. These differences lie not so much in the activities performed, however, as in the techniques used by the training supervisors in performing the activities. This contention is supported by the statements of student teachers relating to their experiences in student teaching. These statements show that the growth of the novice as a teacher is contingent chiefly upon the friendly and cordial atmosphere in which he works and the extent to which he feels free to throw his energy, effort, and understanding into his work.

CHAPTER VI

AN ANALYSIS OF THE SUPERVISORY TECHNIQUES OF THE TRAINING SUPERVISOR

The supervisory techniques reported in this chapter were gathered from two groups of supervisors, designated for convenience as Groups I and II. The seventeen supervisors making up the first group were working in the training schools of the normal schools and teachers colleges which the writer visited while distributing the check lists of supervisory activities. The thirteen supervisors making up the second group were graduate students in Teachers College, Columbia University, who were taking a course dealing with training school problems. All of the latter group had had considerable experience in supervision of student teaching and were making further preparation to continue in such work. Since both groups were asked to give what they regarded as their best techniques, the data reported in this chapter may be regarded as a sampling of the better supervisory techniques which are being used at the present time in training schools throughout the country.

TECHNIQUES REPORTED BY GROUP I

To each supervisor explanation was made of the purpose and method of the study which the writer was making and the help of the supervisor was solicited. The following five questions were put orally to each supervisor, the writer recording the answers given:

1. What is the important opportunity which a student teacher meets who comes to your classroom to do his student teaching?
2. How do you help the student teacher to learn to plan lessons?
3. How do you help the student teacher to select and organize subject matter?
4. How do you teach the student teacher to analyze teaching?
5. How do you carry on your conferences with student teachers?

These questions were answered in varying detail by seventeen supervisors of student teaching.[1]

One supervisor, in reply to the first question, said that her classroom gave the student teacher the opportunity

> To assume responsibility; to feel himself a part of things; to come to have a notion of what the teaching task is; to work with a group of children who are trying to learn to direct their own thinking, planning, and work; and to come to have a sympathetic and coöperative feeling toward such children. I ask the student to try to forget me. I have been as he is and I know how he feels. I tell him to be himself and to let the children be themselves. I ask him to try to discover his points of strength and of weakness. After some observation and participation I ask him to write a rather complete statement of what he thinks he can do and what he thinks he cannot do; and what characteristics of manner and voice he feels he needs to try to acquire. Our problem then becomes: How go about acquiring these things which he lacks?

A summary of all the replies of the supervisors to the first question shows that the supervisors differ somewhat in their conceptions of the opportunity which the student teacher meets when he comes to their classrooms to do his student teaching. Their replies mention fourteen different items. Working with children is mentioned 11 times; studying teaching, 5; being responsible for the work with children, 4; working *with* an experienced teacher, 3; teaching under supervision, 3; being directed so that the first teaching is successful, 3; being helped in acquiring teaching personality, 3; studying the educational theory which underlies the teaching, 2; trying out theories and principles learned in college, 2; analyzing oneself as a prospective teacher, 2; learning to select and organize subject matter, 2. Other items mentioned once each are: being guided in the study of children at work and at play, participating in health work, and being held constantly to a high standard of attainment.

Of the fourteen items, only three indicate that the supervisors tend to think of the student teacher's opportunity as including types of extra-class activities. These three items are mentioned but once each. The items show that supervisors do believe that student teachers should work with children. The items, the student teacher being responsible for the work with the children and being directed so that the first teaching is successful, have the respective frequencies of 4 and 3. These are evidences that the supervisors do look upon the student teacher as a co-worker.

[1] For a complete statement of the replies see Appendix E, p. 108.

Two rather different types of replies to the question dealing with lesson planning are as follows:

> I permit the student teacher to make the type of plan he wants to make. The only requirement is that the plan be his best preparation to teach. I have found that formal plans prevent the teacher from *teaching* the children. Informal planning helps to cultivate a desirable teacher-pupil relationship. I ask him to indicate in his plan enough to make clear what he plans to do. We use unit plans rather than daily plans. The daily connections are indicated in the unit plan by means of a colored pencil.

> I give the student plans for all lessons which I ask him specifically to observe. This permits him to follow each step of the lesson as the teaching proceeds. I ask him to make notes of all points which he wants to discuss in conference. At first he has few points to discuss. I then put questions to him. We continue this until he is able to discuss the lessons observed from the standpoint of the plans and to raise questions. I cover each type of lesson in this way—drill, information, problem-solving, and appreciation. Then the student may refer to these plans when he teaches. I urge him to use his own ideas when he plans and not copy only.

Examination of the seventeen techniques used in teaching lesson planning indicates that the supervisors, as a group, are rather formal in their lesson planning. One supervisor frankly says,

> I require rather definite planning covering teacher and pupil aims, introduction or point of contact with earlier work, procedure, and conclusion or summary. I ask the student to be rather definite in the beginning.

Only two supervisors have techniques which seem to be informal. One supervisor says,

> I do not have the student teacher write lesson plans as such. It takes the time which the student needs to spend on his preparation for his work with the children. . . . I do have the student write out the important test questions which he plans to ask the children.

The other supervisor says,

> I permit the student teacher to make the type of plan he wants to make. The only requirement is that it be his best preparation to teach.

There are evidences, however, that a larger number of the supervisors would like to be less formal in their work, for seven of them indicate that they want the student to be free to use his own ideas.

Unit lesson plans are used by thirteen supervisors; detailed lesson plans at the first of the term and less detailed at the end of the term are used by seven; daily lesson plans are used for at least a part of the term by four supervisors.[2]

One supervisor in reply to the question concerning teaching selection and organization of subject matter says:

> I have a classified collection of teaching materials which I have been gathering for many years. I show this to the student teacher and tell him how I have collected it. I suggest to him to do the same thing. We make a great deal of use of my collection so he sees its value. I ask the children to bring in material which they find outside of school and which interests them. Much of this is valuable material and I add it to my collection in case the children do not wish to keep it. I try to help the student to acquire standards for judging such material so that he may know what to keep and what to throw away. We take many excursions. The student teacher goes first and selects the places which we shall visit. The things which we see and find and bring back to school with us serve as a basis for many oral and written language, geography, and history lessons. The student learns that the excursion needs careful planning and handling if it is to provide educative experiences for the children.

A summary of all the replies by the supervisors to the third question gives a total mention of thirteen different ways of teaching student teachers to select and organize teaching materials. The item, show student teacher collections of materials and have student use these, is mentioned 8 times; teaching student teacher to select and organize teaching materials is a hard problem, is mentioned 5 times; tell student teacher how to obtain and file teaching materials, 5; take school excursions, 5; direct children to bring materials, 5; use libraries, 5; plan projects which involve collecting materials, 3; ask student teachers to gather pictures, stories, and poems to supplement the text books, 2; help students to acquire standards for evaluating teaching materials, 2; show need for supplementary materials, 2; show what former student teachers have done, 1; urge student teacher to bring in supplementary material for each lesson, 1; and ask student teacher to watch local papers for items of local history and geography, 1.

The above array of items is varied enough to show that many student teachers should be learning to become more than textbook teachers. These items indicate that student teachers are having some experiences which will help them to do constructive work

---

[2] A summary treatment of the techniques in teaching lesson planning is rather inadequate. For the complete statement of these techniques, the reader should refer to Appendix E, pp. 110–113.

along these lines. The fact that five supervisors frankly state that it is hard to teach the student teacher to select and to organize teaching materials reveals the strength of the grip which formal textbook teaching has upon us.

The fourth question asked how the supervisors taught the student teacher to analyze teaching. One supervisor replied:

> I want the student to learn to analyze himself and his teaching and to come to see both his strong and his weak points. I ask him what he is doing each month for himself and what purposes lie back of what he is doing. We work out a list of things which he wants to accomplish and we aim directly at a few of the simpler ones first. We do not attempt too much at a time as it is essential that progress be made. As time goes on we add to the list of things to be accomplished. The student must check himself to see the progress which he is making. I also ask the student to analyze in writing each lesson he teaches before coming to see me for a conference. We then compare and the student has to decide what is to be done.

Other techniques used by supervisors, together with the respective frequencies of these techniques are: teach student teacher to analyze his own teaching and that of supervisor, 15; analyze to see what the children have learned, 3; and use a rating form, discussing each point on the form with the student teacher, 3. Other techniques mentioned once each are: student teacher lists qualities of good personality and then checks himself to see which ones are lacking; supervisor writes a daily criticism which is given to the student; supervisor tries to be best possible personal example for student teacher; supervisor makes a list of things which student is to accomplish; supervisor asks student to recall teachers whom he has had and thinks good and then to compare himself with these teachers in personal qualities; student uses informal objective tests to reveal results of the teaching.

This summary of the techniques used to cultivate in the student teacher the habit of analysis does not reveal clearly enough the objectives of the supervisor. All efforts to help the student teacher acquire the habit of analyzing teaching should be vigorously pointed toward a knowledge and an understanding of the psychological principles which underlie successful teaching and successful treatment of the problem of individual differences.

Analysis of the techniques used by the supervisors in carrying on the conferences with the student teachers shows that supervisors realize the importance and value of the conferences.

The general practice of the seventeen supervisors answering the question relating to conferences is to hold both general and individual conferences. The general conferences tend to be regularly scheduled while the individual ones are held when occasion demands. There is some tendency on the part of supervisors to place the responsibility for the content of the conferences upon the student teachers. One supervisor tries

> to leave the content and time of holding the individual conference to the individual student teacher.

Another leaves

> the responsibility for the content of both the group and individual conferences largely to the student teacher.

Another tendency is to take up in the conferences only topics which will help the students with the problems that are giving them the most trouble. The statements of the techniques used have little evidence in them to indicate that student teachers bring to the conference objective data for the procedures which they are using in their work with the pupils. Only three supervisors are clearly working along this line. One supervisor states that she "asks each student to be ready with his opinion as to what pupil changes we should try to make . . . and to have objective evidence for his opinion." A second supervisor reports the consideration of diagnostic progress charts for the children. A third says that a study is made of the children "with a view to learning their interests, needs, and abilities. This is done by examining tests which we have given the children." While it may be that supervisors are doing more along this line than these statements of techniques indicate it is likely that many student teachers are not learning that we must have objective evidence to use as a basis if our analysis of teaching is to be sound.

TECHNIQUES REPORTED BY GROUP II

Copies of the check list of supervisory activities were distributed to the students in Group II with the request that they write out in sufficient detail to make their procedure clear what they consider their best technique for the performance of any one of the activities of the check list. Thirteen students responded to this request. The techniques which they submitted, together with the activities to which the techniques belonged, are given in the Appendix.[3]

An accurate evaluation of any one of these techniques reported in Appendix E would involve having a definite training situation in mind. One should know what facilities are available in the training school for having the particular technique used, how long a term and how long a day the student teacher stays in the training school, and what has been the content of courses the student teacher has had prior to undertaking his student teaching. These will vary in different teacher-training schools. This evaluation will also be conditioned, in a measure, by the needs and opportunities the prospective teachers will meet when they go out to teach. On the other hand, students of teacher training have set up standards which can be used as a means for evaluating supervisory techniques.

Armentrout[4] holds that the student teacher is a laboratory worker who is trying to find out the psychological and educational principles underlying the learning and the teaching process and that all supervisory techniques must be such that the student teacher is stimulated to discover these principles rather than merely to see the specific devices and methods used in a particular lesson.

Charters and Waples[5] determined five progressive levels of depth to be used in evaluating activities. These levels of depth are as follows:

Depth	Interpretation
1	The activity is merely mentioned.
2	The activity is described in sufficient detail to make its meaning clear to students unfamiliar with it.
3	The activity is discussed to the end of defining difficulties met in performing it.
4	The activity is discussed to show methods of overcoming its difficulties.
5	The activity is discussed with sufficient thoroughness to define principles that support accepted methods of performing it.

Both the Armentrout and the Charters and Waples studies advocate techniques which will insure that the student discovers the underlying psychological and educational principles. Charters and

---

[3] See Appendix E, pp. 120–128.
[4] Armentrout, W. D., *The Conduct of Student Teaching in State Teachers Colleges*, pp. 56–57.
[5] Charters, W. W. and Waples, D., *The Commonwealth Teacher-Training Study*, p. 156. Reprinted by permission of The University of Chicago Press.

Waples would also have the technique of such nature that specific difficulties likely to be met in using it are made known and that methods of overcoming these difficulties are learned.

Examination of the supervisory techniques given in Appendix E reveals that supervisors reporting these techniques are tending to think of the points made by Armentrout and by Charters and Waples.

SUMMARY

Ninety-eight supervisory techniques have been reported in Chapter VI and in Appendix E in sufficient detail to make clear the method of the supervisor in using the technique. We should have recorded in educational literature the best techniques which are being used by supervisors in the various teacher-training institutions of the country. Then the prospective teacher may analyze these techniques in the light of the principles advocated by students of teacher-training problems. This experience will give the prospective teacher a fair stock of teaching techniques which will enable him to attain some degree of teaching success in his first year. In addition it will give the student such an understanding of principles of good teaching that he will be able to work out newer and more effective teaching techniques as he teaches.

CHAPTER VII

SUMMARY, CONCLUSIONS, AND RECOMMENDATIONS

Summary

In this study an attempt has been made to do two things:

1. To determine and analyze the activities of the elementary school training supervisor in working with student teachers.
2. To determine and analyze the techniques of the elementary school training supervisor in carrying on these activities.

To show that training supervisors are able to give reliable information essential to the two problems of the study, data relating to their training and experience were gathered. The data setting forth the facts of training and of experience for 355 training supervisors reveal the following conditions and tendencies:

1. Elementary school supervisors of student teaching, in large numbers, have undertaken their work with little or no *specific* training for it.
2. Approximately 15 per cent of the supervisors contributing data for the study failed or were unable to give names of courses which they had taken and which had given specific help in carrying on work with student teachers.
3. Approximately 85 per cent of the supervisors mentioned more frequently, as having given them specific help in work with student teachers, courses dealing with principles of supervision, principles of education, psychology, and methods, and mentioned less frequently courses dealing with subject matter, the teaching of subject matter, and school administration.
4. Approximately 56 per cent of the supervisors mentioned more frequently, as what they wished they might have taken prior to undertaking supervision of student teaching, courses in principles of supervision, principles of education, and psychology, and less frequently courses in subject matter.

The topics which the supervisors would have had the courses in supervision, education, and psychology treat are:

(1) Conferences with student teacher.
(2) Curriculum construction.
(3) Rating of student teacher.
(4) Essentials of good supervision of student teaching.
(5) Application of psychology to work of training supervisor.
(6) Personality as a factor in teaching.
(7) How meet individual needs of student teacher.
(8) Technique of teaching.
(9) Study of the position and work of the training supervisor.
(10) Bibliographies for student teachers and training supervisors.
(11) Directed observation and discussion of lessons observed.
(12) Discipline problems.
(13) Mental hygiene.
(14) Classroom management.
(15) Health education.
(16) Principles of education.

5. Approximately 50 per cent of the supervisors held the two-year normal school diploma as their highest diploma. Approximately 37 per cent held the bachelor's degree, 12 per cent the master's degree and 0.56 per cent the doctor's degree.

6. Approximately 50 per cent of the supervisors had had from 2 to 3 years of training beyond high school and one half had had 4 years or more of training beyond high school. The median number of years of training beyond high school was 4.0 years.

7. The training supervisors, as a group, were experienced school people. The median length of total school experience was 13.8 years and the median length of experience in supervision of student teaching was 4.9 years.

8. The supervisors had experienced all types of teaching, from kindergarten to university teaching, and had served successfully in all phases of public school administrative work prior to undertaking the supervision of student teaching.

These facts of training and of experience indicate that the supervisors are competent to give suggestions with reference to their work.

To accomplish the first purpose of the study, a check list of 422 supervisory activities was prepared. The check list, in its final form, consists of six sections. These sections, and the number of activities in each section, are as follows: Section I, Supervisory Activities Relating to Children, 70; Section II, Supervisory Activities Relating to Student Teachers, 70; Section III, Supervisory Activities Relating to Teaching, 138; Section IV, Supervisory Activities Relating to School and Classroom Management, 77; Section V, Supervisory Activities Relating to Administration of Student Teaching Program, 35; and Section VI, Miscellaneous Supervisory Activities, 32.

Three hundred fifty-five elementary school supervisors of student teaching, working in forty-five state normal schools and teachers colleges of twenty-eight states, rated the activities of the check list from the standpoint of three criteria: (1) *Frequency of performance*; (2) *need for training*; and (3) *value to the student teacher*. Decile ranks of the activities of the check list according to each criterion were computed. These decile ranks were numbered from 1 to 10, 1 being the lowest and 10 the highest decile. More than 75 per cent of the activities of the third section (activities relating to teaching) are in the upper 5 decile ranks according to all three criteria. Forty per cent of the activities of the first section (activities relating to children) are in the upper 5 decile ranks according to *frequency of performance*; 68 per cent are in the upper 5 decile ranks according to *need for training*; and 53 per cent are in the upper 5 decile ranks according to *value to the student teacher*. Thirty-seven per cent of the activities of the second section (activities relating to student teachers) are in the upper 5 decile ranks according to *frequency of performance*; 64 per cent are in the upper 5 decile ranks according to *need for training*; and 40 per cent are in the upper 5 decile ranks according to *value to the student teacher*. Twenty-six per cent of the activities of the fourth section (activities relating to school and classroom management) are in the upper 5 decile ranks according to *frequency of performance*; 14 per cent are in the upper 5 decile ranks according to *need for training*; and 18 per cent are in the upper 5 decile ranks according to *value to the student teacher*.

Forty-eight per cent of the activities of the fifth section (activities relating to administration of the student teaching program) are in the upper 5 decile ranks according to *frequency of performance*; 17 per cent are in the upper 5 decile ranks according to *need for training*; and 37 per cent are in the upper 5 decile ranks according to *value to the student teacher*. Twenty-eight per cent of the activities of the sixth section (miscellaneous activities) are in the upper 5 decile ranks according to *frequency of performance*; none is in the upper 5 decile ranks according to *need for training*; and 31 per cent are in the upper 5 decile ranks according to *value to the student teacher*.

The interest of supervisors, when *frequency of performance* is considered, is first in activities relating to teaching, second in activities relating to administration of the student teaching program, third in activities relating to children, fourth in activities relating to student teachers, fifth in the miscellaneous group of activities, and sixth in activities relating to school and classroom management. The interest of supervisors, when *need for training* is considered, is first in the activities relating to teaching, second in activities relating to children, third in activities relating to student teachers, fourth in activities relating to administration of the student teaching program, fifth in activities relating to school and classroom management, and sixth in the miscellaneous group of activities. The interest of supervisors, when *value to the student teacher* is considered, is first in activities relating to teaching, second in activities relating to children, third in activities relating to student teachers, fourth in activities relating to administration, fifth in the miscellaneous group of activities, and sixth in activities relating to school and classroom management. In general, the interest of supervisors is first in teaching, second in children, third in student teachers, fourth in administration of the program of student teaching, fifth in the miscellaneous group of activities, and sixth in school and classroom management.

Analysis of the particular activities which training supervisors are performing reveals that student teachers tend not to have opportunities to do the following things:

1. To become acquainted with the children except in the classroom.
2. To have contacts with programs of health and physical education for children.

3. To learn to use standardized intelligence and achievement tests in connection with teaching.
4. To take children on school excursions.
5. To supervise children in their preparation for school programs and school parties.
6. To handle office records and reports.
7. To participate in meetings of parent-teachers' associations.

In general the contacts of the student teachers in their student teaching experiences are limited to the classroom teaching.

As a check upon the analysis of the activities which training supervisors perform in their work with student teaching, statements dealing with their experiences in student teaching were obtained from 411 student teachers in six state normal schools and teachers colleges. These statements show that the growth which a student makes as a teacher depends just as much upon the relation existing between him and his supervisor and the extent to which he feels free to throw his energy and understanding into the work as it does upon what he does.

As a basis for determining and analyzing the techniques used by supervisors in carrying on their work with student teachers, eighty-five techniques were obtained from supervisors in ten normal schools and teachers colleges and thirteen techniques were obtained from graduate students attending Teachers College, Columbia University.[1] The techniques obtained from the supervisors relate to the following: the opportunity which a student teacher has; teaching of lesson planning; teaching of the selection and organization of subject matter; teaching of analysis of teaching; and conducting of conferences. The techniques obtained from the graduate students relate to certain activities of the check list.

The techniques show that supervisors tend to be rather formal in their work. On the other hand, there is evidence that the supervisors are trying to help the student teacher see the psychological and educational principles which underlie teaching and are giving him a chance to use his own ideas.

Conclusions and Recommendations

The analysis of supervisory activities and techniques of training supervisors reveals that student teachers are having a rather

---

[1] The reader wishing to see these techniques is referred to Appendix E, p. 108.

limited experience. This limited experience is due, obviously, to many circumstances and conditions. Improvement of the program of student teaching must be made with due consideration of these circumstances and conditions. To guide this consideration an attempt has been made to evolve some principles, based upon the findings of this study and upon educational theory. The following represent the results of this attempt:

1. Teaching should be regarded as one of the finest types of human relationships. It enables immaturity, with the guidance and help of maturity, most nearly to realize its highest potentialities.
2. Supervision, whether in the public school and with teachers in service, or in the training school and with student teachers, is a type of teaching and must recognize the purposes and responsibilities of the person being supervised.
3. Successful teaching in any teaching level requires a teacher personally fitted and specifically trained for the type of work to be done.
4. The objective of a student-teaching program is to introduce the student teacher to the whole teaching task.
5. The psychology of individual differences applies to the teaching of teachers just as well as to the teaching of children.

In the light of these principles certain comments with respect to the program of student teaching and the staff carrying on the program may be made.

Training supervisors should be a selected group, selected for personal qualities and for skill in teaching. They should have a year of graduate training, the courses of which are not prescribed in advance but are prescribed so as to meet their peculiar needs and to give the specific training necessary to enable the teacher to become a supervisor of student teachers. A part of this training should involve laboratory experience which gives the prospective supervisor the opportunity of supervising student teachers under the guidance of an expert supervisor of student teaching.[2]

The program of work for the student teacher should be the outgrowth, in part, of his own thinking and planning. The growth

[2] The writer is indebted to Professor Thomas Alexander for the idea contained in the foregoing. Professor Alexander now has at Teachers College, Columbia University, a program for the training of supervisors of student teaching, which is based on this idea.

of the student teacher will vary directly with his opportunity to share constructively in the planning of this program.

This program must be based upon a recognition of the fact that the teaching task is not confined to the classroom. Instead, it involves all the work of the school with the pupils. The program should give the student teacher opportunity to engage in all the activities of the best teacher in the best progressive school. Only when this end has been attained has the program of student teaching been well planned.

APPENDIX

A

A CHECK LIST OF THE SUPERVISORY ACTIVITIES OF THE ELEMENTARY SCHOOL TRAINING SUPERVISOR IN STATE NORMAL SCHOOLS AND TEACHERS COLLEGES

To All Persons Who Supervise Student Teachers in the Elementary Grades:

I am making a study of the supervisory activities of the elementary school training supervisor. In the study the term *elementary school training supervisor* is used to mean any person who, either in the campus training school or affiliated public school, supervises student teachers working in any of the first eight grades. It is thought that the study will help to define just what the work of the elementary school training supervisor should be.

It is realized that no one having a part in the teacher-training program is busier than the training supervisor. The facts relating to the supervision of student teachers can be learned best, however, only from those who do the work.

Will you, therefore, help me in this study by doing two things? First, give the personal data asked for; second, check the items of the check list according to the instructions. Please be sure to give your name so as to permit sending you a letter of inquiry in case further information from you in regard to your check list should prove necessary. All the information obtained will be treated in a wholly impersonal manner and so reported that individuals cannot be identified.

Please give the information asked for and check the items of the check list at your earliest opportunity. Then place the check list in the enclosed, stamped, and addressed envelope and mail at once. I wish very much to have the check list checked by all the elementary school training supervisors of your institution. Please fill out the check list and return as soon as possible. Your coöperation will be greatly appreciated.

Very truly yours,

HARRY N. FITCH
509 West 121st Street
New York City

A. PERSONAL DATA

Please fill out all blanks

Name of person reporting ....
Name and location of institution ....

I. TRAINING OF PERSON REPORTING

KIND OF SCHOOL	NUMBER OF YEARS ATTENDED	NUMBER OF SUMMERS ATTENDED	DIPLOMA OR DEGREE
High School	....	....	....
Normal School or Teachers College	....	....	....
College	....	....	....
University	....	....	....

Give names of courses you have taken which have been of *specific* help to you in your work with student teachers:

NAME OF COURSES	WHERE TAKEN
....	....
....	....
....	....
....	....
....	....
....	....
....	....
....	....
....	....
....	....
....	....
....	....
....	....
....	....
....	....
....	....
....	....
....	....
....	....
....	....

Have you ever thought of a course which you wish you might have taken before undertaking the supervision of student teachers?
Yes .... No ....
Suggest name for course ....
Mention three topics which you would want this course to treat:

1. ....
2. ....
3. ....

II. EXPERIENCE OF PERSON REPORTING

Total years taught ....; years as classroom teacher only ....; years as critic teacher or as training supervisor ....; years in other school work .... Total number of student teachers you have supervised* ....; number of student teachers you are supervising now .... Position held now ....
In campus training school? ....; in affiliated public school? ....
Please list positions you have held and give years spent in each.

(*E.g.*, primary teacher—three years; high school teacher—two years.)

POSITIONS HELD

....
....
....
....
....
....

B. LIST OF THE SUPERVISORY ACTIVITIES OF THE ELEMENTARY SCHOOL TRAINING SUPERVISOR

Important: To secure uniform results, please do the following things, *one* at a time, and in the *order given*.

First: In Column 1, place 1, 2, 3, or 4 after each activity which you perform to show the frequency of performance in your work with student teachers, placing 1 after each activity which you perform frequently, 2 after each activity which you perform less frequently, 3 after each activity which you perform least frequently, and 4 after each activity which you do not perform at all.

Training Supervisors Are Not Expected to Perform All of These Activities

Second: In Column 2, place X after each activity in which you think the training supervisor should have training before taking up the job. It is assumed that those activities left unchecked in this column are ones which you think may be learned easily by the training supervisor on the job. Consider all the activities whether you perform them or not.

Third: In Column 3, place 1, 2, or 3 after each activity to show what you think is its value in the training of the student teacher. Place 1 after each activity of better than average value, 2 after each activity of average value, and 3 after each activity of less than average value. Consider all the activities.

* Estimate, if necessary.

I. SUPERVISORY ACTIVITIES RELATING TO CHILDREN

	Col. 1	Col. 2	Col. 3
1. Create in children proper attitude toward student teacher	....	....	....
2. Bear responsibility for progress of children	....	....	....
3. See that pupils do not suffer from inaccuracies of student teacher	....	....	....
4. Supplement teaching of student teacher for sake of thoroughness	....	....	....
5. Direct student teacher to study habits of children	....	....	....
6. Direct student teacher to classify habits of children	....	....	....
7. Direct student teacher to study children as a group	....	....	....
8. Direct student teacher to study children as individuals	....	....	....
9. Direct student teacher to study mental characteristics of children	....	....	....
10. Direct student teacher to classify mental characteristics of children	....	....	....
11. Direct student teacher to study personal characteristics of children	....	....	....
12. Direct student teacher to classify personal characteristics of children	....	....	....
13. Direct student teacher to study interests of children	....	....	....
14. Direct student teacher to classify interests of children	....	....	....
15. Direct student teacher to study social attitudes of children	....	....	....
16. Direct student teacher to classify social attitudes of children	....	....	....
17. Direct student teacher in giving intelligence tests	....	....	....
18. Supervise student teacher in scoring intelligence tests	....	....	....
19. Supervise student teacher in tabulating results of intelligence tests	....	....	....
20. Teach student teacher to make usable records of intelligence tests results	....	....	....
21. Teach student teacher to make use of intelligence scores in planning work	....	....	....
22. Direct student teacher in giving achievement tests to children	....	....	....
23. Supervise student teacher in scoring achievement tests	....	....	....
24. Supervise student teacher in tabulating results of achievement tests	....	....	....
25. Teach student teacher to make usable records of achievement tests results	....	....	....
26. Teach student teacher to use achievement tests scores in planning work	....	....	....
27. Help student teacher to plan conference with child who has unsocial attitude	....	....	....
28. Teach student teacher to hold conference with child who has unsocial attitude	....	....	....
29. Help student teacher to plan "follow-up" conferences with child who has unsocial attitude	....	....	....
30. Teach student teacher to hold "follow-up" conferences with child who has unsocial attitude	....	....	....
31. Direct student teacher to inspect children for evidences of communicable diseases	....	....	....
32. Direct student teacher to inspect children for evidences of malnutrition	....	....	....
33. Direct student teacher to inspect children for evidences of defective hearing	....	....	....
34. Direct student teacher to inspect children for evidences of defective vision	....	....	....
35. Direct student teacher to inspect children for evidences of defective teeth	....	....	....
36. Direct student teacher to inspect children for evidences of diseased tonsils	....	....	....
37. Direct student teacher to inspect children for evidences of adenoids	....	....	....
38. Direct student teacher to inspect children for evidences of poor posture	....	....	....
39. Direct student teacher to weigh children	....	....	....
40. Direct student teacher to measure heights of children	....	....	....
41. Direct student teacher to secure accurate ages of children	....	....	....
42. Direct student teacher to inspect children for evidences of nervousness	....	....	....
43. Teach student teacher to aid children who stutter and stammer	....	....	....
44. Teach student teacher to treat child who is left-handed	....	....	....
45. Teach student teacher to make usable records of facts relating to physical condition	....	....	....
46. Direct student teacher to make a health survey of children	....	....	....
47. Teach student teacher what teacher's responsibility for health needs of children is	....	....	....
48. Teach student teacher to take care of health needs of pupils	....	....	....

	Col. 1	Col. 2	Col. 3
49. Direct student teacher to handle the case of the tardy child	....	....	....
50. Direct student teacher to handle the case of the habitually absent child	....	....	....
51. Show student teacher necessity of respecting personality of child	....	....	....
52. Teach student teacher how to respect personality of child	....	....	....
53. Require student teacher to handle disciplinary problems when he teaches	....	....	....
54. Advise with student teacher concerning disciplinary problems	....	....	....
55. See that student teacher learns that children must be happy in schoolroom	....	....	....
56. Teach student teacher how to make children happy in schoolroom	....	....	....
57. Train student teacher to check oral work of children	....	....	....
58. Teach student teacher how to grade oral work of children	....	....	....
59. Train student teacher to check written work of children	....	....	....
60. Teach student teacher how to grade written work of children	....	....	....
61. Teach student teacher how to study home life of children	....	....	....
62. Train student teacher to keep in touch with parents of children	....	....	....
63. Train student teacher to keep parents informed of progress of children	....	....	....
64. Teach student teacher to train children in care of all school supplies	....	....	....
65. Teach student teacher to train children in care of school furniture	....	....	....
66. Teach student teacher to train children in care of school buildings	....	....	....
67. Direct student teacher to hear reports of children on books read	....	....	....
68. Direct student teacher to hear reports of children on poems learned	....	....	....
69. Teach student teacher to provide for moral development of children	....	....	....
70. Visit homes of children with student teacher	....	....	....

Please add to this list any supervisory activities relating to children which you know but which are not included above. Check activities added according to instructions one, two, and three.

	Col. 1	Col. 2	Col. 3
....	....	....	....
....	....	....	....
....	....	....	....
....	....	....	....
....	....	....	....
....	....	....	....
....	....	....	....
....	....	....	....

II. SUPERVISORY ACTIVITIES RELATING TO STUDENT TEACHER

	Col. 1	Col. 2	Col. 3
1. Create in student teacher proper attitude toward children	....	....	....
2. Create in student teacher proper attitude toward his work as student teacher		....	....
3. Teach student teacher to make an analysis of himself as a prospective teacher		....	....
4. Direct student teacher to analyze his writing from standpoint of ease of reading by children		....	....
5. Direct student teacher to analyze his writing from standpoint of system being taught children		....	....
6. Teach student teacher to be attentive to his own oral English	....	....	....
7. Teach student teacher to be attentive to his own written English	....	....	....
8. Train student teacher in habit of correcting his own oral English	....	....	....
9. Train student teacher in habit of correcting his own written English	....	....	....
10. Teach student teacher to study objectively his own achievement in school subjects		....	....
11. Show student teacher ways of improving his knowledge of school subjects	....	....	....

	Col. 1	Col. 2	Col. 3

12. Show student teacher necessity of constant effort to improve his knowledge of subject matter ....

13. Teach student teacher how to study ....

14. Direct student teacher in study of qualities making up best teaching personality ....

15. Advise with student teacher in matters of dress ....

16. Advise with student teacher in matters of personal cleanliness ....

17. Advise with student teacher with respect to poise of mind when standing before class ....

18. Advise with student teacher with respect to poise of body when standing before class ....

19. Direct student teacher to develop a good teaching voice ....

20. Train student teacher in ways of conserving his vitality ....

21. Stimulate and encourage student teacher ....

22. Advise with student teacher as to how to be at ease when meeting people

23. Advise with student teacher as to how to help others to be at ease when he is meeting them ....

24. Advise with student teacher as to how to acquire self-confidence ....

25. Advise with student teacher as to how to be tactful when dealing with parents ....

26. Advise with student teacher as to how to be tactful when dealing with children ....

27. Teach student teacher what sincerity on part of teacher involves ......

28. Teach student teacher why teacher must be judicious in choosing associates ....

29. Help student teacher to develop professional attitudes ....

30. Help student teacher to work out a professional code of ethics ....

31. Make student teacher feel at home in classroom ....

32. Respect opinions of student teacher ....

33. Have such relation to student teacher that he is always at his best when with supervisor ....

34. Create in student teacher proper attitude toward school community ....

35. Teach student teacher subject matter which he later teaches to children

36. Confer with student teacher who wishes help in preparation of lesson ...

37. Teach student teacher how to take notes ....

38. Require student teacher to write observation reports for all lessons observed ....

39. Require student teacher to write observation reports for some of the lessons observed ....

40. Require student teacher to write observation reports for all demonstration lessons observed ....

41. Require student teacher to write observation reports for some of the demonstration lessons observed ....

42. Give student teacher outline to guide his observations ....

43. Give student teacher questions to answer in reporting his observations

44. Correct observation reports ....

45. Grade observation reports before returning to student teacher ....

46. Discuss observation reports with student teacher ....

47. Check all work graded by student teacher ....

48. Frequently check work graded by student teacher ....

49. Tell student teacher of valuable references ....

50. Assign regular reference-reading to student teacher ....

51. Require student teacher to hand in notes on readings ....

52. Grade student teacher's notes on readings ....

53. Discuss with student teacher his notes on readings ....

54. Discuss with student teacher topics suggested by supervisor's study of music, art, and literature ....

55. Adjust misunderstandings which have arisen between student teacher and children ....

	Col. 1	Col. 2	Col. 3
56. Discuss with student teacher points raised by director of training in general conference	....	....	....
57. Keep a detailed record of student teacher's progress	....	....	....
58. Keep a detailed record of student teacher's needs	....	....	....
59. Require student teacher to keep a detailed record of his own progress	....	....	....
60. Require student teacher to keep a detailed record of his own needs	....	....	....
61. Put forth more effort to improve good student teacher than poor one	....	....	....
62. Put forth more effort to improve poor student teacher than good one	....	....	....
63. Rate student teacher on some rating scale	....	....	....
64. Require student teacher to rate himself on some rating scale	....	....	....
65. Compare supervisor's ratings with those of student teacher	....	....	....
66. Discuss ratings with student teacher	....	....	....
67. Show student teacher how to take objectively suggestions for improvement	....	....	....
68. Vary weekly program to care for individual differences of student teachers	....	....	....
69. Entertain student teacher at supervisor's home	....	....	....
70. Entertain student teacher elsewhere	....	....	....

Please add to this list any supervisory activities relating to student teachers which you know but which are not included above. Check activities added according to instructions one, two, and three.

	Col. 1	Col. 2	Col. 3
....	....	....	....
....	....	....	....
....	....	....	....
....	....	....	....
....	....	....	....
....	....	....	....
....	....	....	....
....	....	....	....

III. SUPERVISORY ACTIVITIES RELATING TO TEACHING

	Col. 1	Col. 2	Col. 3
1. Teach student teacher to make lesson plans	....	....	....
2. Show student teacher relation of lesson plans to larger objectives of the school	....	....	....
3. Discuss lesson aims with student teacher	....	....	....
4. Teach student teacher to consider experiences of children in planning lessons	....	....	....
5. Teach student teacher to consider needs of children in planning lessons	....	....	....
6. Teach student teacher to consider interests of children in planning lessons	....	....	....
7. Teach student teacher to consider abilities of children in planning lessons	....	....	....
8. Teach student teacher to discover pupil experiences appropriate for lesson to be taught	....	....	....
9. Teach student teacher to use pupil experiences appropriate for lesson to be taught	....	....	....
10. Direct student teacher to gather experiences from everyday life to vitalize subject matter of lesson	....	....	....
11. Teach student teacher to see that lesson provides for pupil motive	....	....	....
12. Teach student teacher to watch for original or creative work by children	....	....	....
13. Teach student teacher to keep records of original or creative work by children	....	....	....
14. Teach student teacher to discover factors influencing child to do original piece of work	....	....	....
15. Teach student teacher to analyze teaching from standpoint of plan	....	....	....

	Col. 1	Col. 2	Col. 3
16. Correct student teacher's lesson plan			
17. Grade student teacher's lesson plan			
18. Discuss corrections made in lesson plan with student teacher			
19. Provide a natural teaching situation for student teacher's first lessons			
20. Help student teacher in planning units of work			
21. Plan work for the student teacher to organize and work out for himself			
22. Train student teacher to test everything he plans from standpoint of children's needs			
23. Train student teacher to test everything he plans from standpoint of children's interests			
24. Train student teacher to test everything he plans from standpoint of children's abilities			
25. Show student teacher that planning is essential to good teaching			
26. Train student teacher to get all supplementary teaching materials ready before he starts to teach the lesson			
27. Show student teacher what preparation for teaching a lesson involves			
28. Teach demonstration lessons for student teacher			
29. Teach student teacher to observe			
30. Teach student teacher to interpret what is observed in terms of the laws of learning			
31. Discuss with student teacher demonstration lessons which he has observed			
32. Plan with student teacher term's work			
33. Observe student teacher when he teaches			
34. After observing student teacher, analyze his teaching procedure carefully before conferring with him			
35. Give student teacher written criticism of his teaching			
36. Discuss his teaching procedure with student teacher			
37. Teach student teacher the place of pupil activity in the lesson			
38. Teach student teacher the place of subject matter in the lesson			
39. Teach student teacher to recognize time and place for testing his teaching			
40. Teach student teacher to test his teaching			
41. Teach student teacher to use standardized tests in connection with his teaching			
42. Teach student teacher to use informal objective tests in connection with his teaching			
43. Direct student teacher to do the necessary "follow-up" teaching with children			
44. Discuss with student teacher the requirements of course of study			
45. Show student teacher that course of study is his guide and aid, not his master			
46. Keep before student teacher the thought that subject matter is a means and not an end			
47. Teach student teacher how to select subject matter			
48. Teach student teacher how to organize subject matter			
49. Give student teacher responsibility for selecting and organizing a complete unit of subject matter			
50. Give student teacher responsibility for teaching a complete unit of subject matter			
51. Teach student teacher to determine what parts of lesson are fundamental			
52. Teach student teacher to determine what parts of lesson are easy for children			
53. Teach student teacher to determine what parts of lesson are hard for children			
54. Train student teacher to analyze his ability to direct pupil's learning activity			
55. Teach student teacher how to determine type of learning activity to be used by pupil in mastery of any kind of subject matter			
56. Teach student teacher to apply psychological principles with respect to individual differences			

	Col. 1	Col. 2	Col. 3

57. Teach student teacher to recognize time and place for different types of assignments ....
58. Teach student teacher how to make different types of assignments .....
59. Teach student teacher to determine what parts of course need different types of treatment ....
60. Show student teacher time and place for socialized classwork ....
61. Show student teacher time and place for individualized work ....
62. Show student teacher time and place for supervised study ....
63. Train student teacher to carry on socialized class work ....
64. Train student teacher to carry on individualized work ....
65. Train student teacher to carry on supervised study ....
66. Show student teacher time and place for drill work ....
67. Show student teacher time and place for problem solving ....
68. Show student teacher time and place for inductive thinking ....
69. Show student teacher time and place for deductive thinking ....
70. Show student teacher time and place for project work ....
71. Show student teacher time and place for dramatization work ....
72. Show student teacher time and place for construction work by children as a means of expression of their ideas ....
73. Show student teacher time and place for creative work by children .....
74. Show student teacher time and place for appreciation lesson ....
75. Train student teacher to carry on drill work ....
76. Train student teacher to carry on problem solving ....
77. Train student teacher to carry on inductive lesson ....
78. Train student teacher to carry on deductive lesson ....
79. Train student teacher to carry on project work ....
80. Train student teacher to carry on dramatization work ....
81. Train student teacher to direct free-construction work by children .....
82. Train student teacher to direct creative work ....
83. Train student teacher to carry on appreciation lesson ....
84. Direct student teacher to study his own questioning ....
85. Teach student teacher to study examples of thinking on part of children
86. Teach student teacher to discover factors influencing thinking on part of children ....
87. Teach student teacher to observe laws of learning in his teaching ......
88. Give questions to student teacher to guide his analysis of his teaching ..
89. Require student teacher to analyze in writing each lesson he teaches ...
90. Require student teacher to analyze in writing some of the lessons he teaches ....
91. Follow a plan of graded introduction to responsible teaching ....
92. Get student teacher to use in his teaching the methods learned in his college or normal school classes ....
93. Teach student teacher how to secure attention of children when he teaches ....
94. Hold student teacher responsible for securing attention of children when he teaches ....
95. Teach student teacher to see the good points in his teaching ....
96. Teach student teacher to see the poor points in his teaching ....
97. Teach student teacher to see why the poor points in his teaching are poor
98. Teach student teacher to see why the good points in his teaching are good ....
99. Train student teacher to hold children responsible for accuracy of facts
100. Hold student teacher responsible for progress of children when he teaches
101. Teach student teacher to test progress of children ....
102. Teach student teacher to make diagnostic records of the work of each pupil ....
103. Teach student teacher how to use diagnostic records of pupils in his teaching ....

	Col. 1	Col. 2	Col. 3
104. Train student teacher to teach pupils to keep their own diagnostic records	....	....	....
105. Train student teacher to hold children responsible for improving their work	....	....	....
106. Hold student teacher responsible for knowing sources of his teaching information	....	....	....
107. Teach student teacher to evaluate sources of teaching information	....	....	....
108. Train student teacher to hold children responsible for knowing sources of their information	....	....	....
109. Train student teacher to teach children to evaluate sources of information	....	....	....
110. Teach student teacher to use community life as a source for teaching materials	....	....	....
111. Teach student teacher to train children in use of textbooks	....	....	....
112. Teach student teacher to train children in use of dictionary	....	....	....
113. Teach student teacher to train children in use of reference books	....	....	....
114. Teach student teacher to train children in use of maps	....	....	....
115. Teach student teacher to train children in use of pictures	....	....	....
116. Teach student teacher to train children in use of card catalog	....	....	....
117. Teach student teacher to train children in use of magazines	....	....	....
118. Teach student teacher to train children in use of newspapers	....	....	....
119. Teach student teacher use of blackboard in class	....	....	....
120. Teach student teacher use of bulletin board	....	....	....
121. Teach student teacher use of lantern and slides	....	....	....
122. Teach student teacher to use visual aids in his teaching	....	....	....
123. Teach student teacher to use verbal illustration in his teaching	....	....	....
124. Teach student teacher to distinguish between method and device	....	....	....
125. Teach student teacher to train children to make a notebook	....	....	....
126. Teach student teacher to train children in use of notebook	....	....	....
127. Direct student teacher to other classrooms to see outstanding pieces of work	....	....	....
128. Teach student teacher to correlate different school subjects	....	....	....
129. Teach student teacher to correlate handwork or construction work with subject matter lessons	....	....	....
130. Direct student teacher to sources of good supplementary teaching materials	....	....	....
131. Teach student teacher to plan school excursion	....	....	....
132. Direct student teacher to visit institutions and places of business to make arrangements for school excursion	....	....	....
133. Teach student teacher to carry out plans for school excursion	....	....	....
134. Teach student teacher to plan opening exercises	....	....	....
135. Teach student teacher to take charge of opening exercises	....	....	....
136. Help student teacher to build up a teaching technique based on psychological principles	....	....	....
137. Direct student teacher to start collecting good teaching materials	....	....	....
138. Direct student teacher to start collecting teaching methods used by good teachers	....	....	....

Please add to this list any supervisory activities relating to teaching which you know but which are not included above. Check activities added according to instructions one, two, and three.

	Col. 1	Col. 2	Col. 3
....	....	....	....
....	....	....	....
....	....	....	....
....	....	....	....
....	....	....	....

	Col.	Col.	Col.
	1	2	3
....	....	....	....
....	....	....	....
....	....	....	....

IV. SUPERVISORY ACTIVITIES RELATING TO SCHOOL AND CLASSROOM MANAGEMENT

	Col.	Col.	Col.
	1	2	3
1. Teach student teacher to care for lighting of classroom	....	....	....
2. Teach student teacher to care for ventilation of classroom	....	....	....
3. Teach student teacher to care for temperature of classroom	....	....	....
4. Teach student teacher to check the seating of children	....	....	....
5. Require student teacher to adjust seats for children	....	....	....
6. Teach student teacher proper placement of all school furniture	....	....	....
7. Teach student teacher to see the principles guiding proper placement of school furniture	....	....	....
8. Teach student teacher to see the principles of caring for physical conditions of classroom	....	....	....
9. Teach student teacher standards as to permanent schoolroom decoration	....	....	....
10. Teach student teacher standards as to temporary schoolroom decoration	....	....	....
11. Teach student teacher to supervise children in decorating classroom for special days	....	....	....
12. Teach student teacher to supervise children in decorating classroom for special weeks	....	....	....
13. Teach student teacher to supervise children in decorating classroom for school parties	....	....	....
14. Teach student teacher to help children plan program for special days	....	....	....
15. Teach student teacher to help children plan program for special weeks	....	....	....
16. Teach student teacher to help children plan program for school parties	....	....	....
17. Teach student teacher to help children carry out plans for special days	....	....	....
18. Teach student teacher to help children carry out program for special weeks	....	....	....
19. Teach student teacher to help children carry out program for school parties	....	....	....
20. Teach student teacher to supervise children's preparation for school programs	....	....	....
21. Train student teacher to direct making of costumes for various occasions	....	....	....
22. Train student teacher to do teacher's part in keeping classroom clean	....	....	....
23. Train student teacher to do teacher's part in keeping school building and yard clean	....	....	....
24. Teach student teacher to train children to be considerate of janitor	....	....	....
25. Teach student teacher to train children in keeping classroom clean	....	....	....
26. Teach student teacher to train children in keeping school building and yard clean	....	....	....
27. Create in student teacher proper attitude toward school janitor	....	....	....
28. Advise with student teacher as to what things a teacher may expect a janitor to do	....	....	....
29. Teach student teacher to inspect toilets	....	....	....
30. Teach student teacher to inspect wardrobes	....	....	....
31. Teach student teacher to inspect children's desks	....	....	....
32. Teach student teacher to inspect children's lockers	....	....	....
33. Require student teacher to report inspections in writing	....	....	....
34. Require student teacher to report inspections orally	....	....	....
35. Discuss with student teacher the report of his inspections	....	....	....
36. Teach student teacher proper procedure if inspections show unfavorable conditions	....	....	....
37. Direct student teacher to wash blackboards	....	....	....
38. Direct student teacher to clean erasers	....	....	....

	Col. 1	Col. 2	Col. 3

39. Direct student teacher to wash windows ....
40. Teach student teacher to supervise washing of windows by children ....
41. Teach student teacher to supervise washing of blackboards by children
42. Teach student teacher to supervise cleaning of erasers by children ....
43. Teach student teacher to supervise children at indoor play ....
44. Teach student teacher to supervise children at play on playground .....
45. Teach student teacher to supervise children going to toilet ....
46. Teach student teacher to supervise children getting a drink ....
47. Teach student teacher to train children as to time for leaving room ....
48. Train student teacher to routinize caring for children's wraps ....
49. Train student teacher to routinize passing of lines ....
50. Train student teacher to do hall duty ....
51. Teach student teacher to supervise children sharpening pencils ....
52. Teach student teacher to keep daily register ....
53. Teach student teacher to keep daily grades of children's work ....
54. Teach student teacher to keep test grades of children's work ....
55. Train student teacher to record children's grades in teacher's record book
56. Train student teacher to fill out children's report book or card ....
57. Give student teacher practice in handling office records ....
58. Check all clerical work done by student teacher ....
59. Train student teacher to take charge of fire drills ....
60. Train student teacher to give first-aid in case of illness ....
61. Train student teacher to give first-aid in case of accidents ....
62. Discuss with student teacher the making of daily program ....
63. Hold student teacher responsible for meeting and dismissing classes on time ....
64. Train student teacher to supervise children's library period ....
65. Train student teacher to supervise children's story hour ....
66. Discuss with student teacher value of parent-teachers' association ....
67. Show student teacher teacher's responsibility with respect to parent-teachers' association ....
68. Give student teacher opportunity to participate in parent-teachers' association ....
69. Give student teacher opportunity to assist with school teas for parents
70. Train student teacher to supplement children's lunch with a hot dish ..
71. Discuss with student teacher values of some form of pupil self-government ....
72. Direct student teacher to study pupil self-government of the classroom
73. Direct student teacher to study pupil self-government of the school ...
74. Give student teacher opportunity to observe the meetings of school council ....
75. Train student teacher to supervise pupil monitors in the classroom ....
76. Show student teacher how to supervise pupil selection of pupil monitors
77. Train student teacher to supervise pupil assignment of duties to pupil monitors ....

Please add to this list any supervisory activities relating to school and classroom management which you know but which are not included above. Check activities added according to instructions one, two, and three.

	Col. 1	Col. 2	Col. 3
....			
....			
....			
....			
....			

	Col. 1	Col. 2	Col. 3
....	....	....	....
....	....	....	....
....	....	....	....

V. SUPERVISORY ACTIVITIES RELATING TO ADMINISTRATION OF STUDENT TEACHING PROGRAM

	Col. 1	Col. 2	Col. 3
1. Attend meetings of supervisors called by director of training	....	....	....
2. Note problems which occur in supervising student teaching	....	....	....
3. Report to director of training problems to be discussed at meetings of training supervisors	....	....	....
4. Attend general conferences of student teachers conducted by director of training	....	....	....
5. Note problems occurring in supervising student teaching which should be taken up in general conferences with student teachers by director of training	....	....	....
6. Report problems to director of training to be discussed at general conferences with student teachers	....	....	....
7. Note points made by director of training at conferences to discuss with student teachers	....	....	....
8. Confer with director of training concerning student teacher whom he has visited	....	....	....
9. Confer with director of training with respect to problems of supervision of student teachers	....	....	....
10. Report to director of training student teacher whose work is below standard	....	....	....
11. Report to director of training student teacher whose work is above standard	....	....	....
12. Report to director of training analysis of reasons for successes of student teachers	....	....	....
13. Report to director of training analysis of reasons for failures of student teachers	....	....	....
14. Report to director of training analysis of the progress of each student teacher each month	....	....	....
15. Report to director of training at end of term detailed statement of student teacher's fitness to teach	....	....	....
16. Grade the teaching of student teacher at end of term	....	....	....
17. Report term grade of student teacher to director of training	....	....	....
18. Report term grade of student teacher to registrar	....	....	....
19. Adjust daily program for director of training to fit student teaching assignments	....	....	....
20. Select student teacher's best lesson plan for filing with director of training	....	....	....
21. Hold individual conferences with student teacher each day	....	....	....
22. Hold individual conferences with student teacher each week	....	....	....
23. Hold group conferences each week with student teachers	....	....	....
24. Hold student teacher responsible for preparing for group conferences	....	....	....
25. Assign topics to student teacher for conference discussion	....	....	....
26. Confer with members of college or normal school faculty as to most helpful prerequisite courses for student teachers	....	....	....
27. Confer with members of college or normal school faculty as to strong points in student teacher's training	....		....
28. Confer with members of college or normal school faculty as to weak points in student teacher's training	....	....	....
29. Confer with subject matter teachers in college or normal school with reference to teaching materials for student teacher	....	....	....

	Col. 1	Col. 2	Col 3
30. Confer with teachers of educational theory in college or normal school with regard to principles of teaching for student teacher	....	....	....
31. Invite members of college or normal school faculty to visit training supervisor's classes	....	....	....
32. Confer with members of college or normal school faculty who have visited supervisor's classes with respect to the teaching	....	....	....
33. Confer with members of college or normal school faculty who have visited supervisor's classes with respect to subject matter being used ...	....	....	....
34. Visit classes taught by members of college or normal school faculty	....	....	....
35. Confer with members of college or normal school faculty with regard to their courses	....	....	....

Please add to this list any supervisory activities relating to administration of student teaching program which you know but which are not included above. Check activities added according to instructions one, two, and three.

	Col. 1	Col. 2	Col. 3
....	....	....	....
....	....	....	....
....	....	....	....
....	....	....	....
....	....	....	....
....	....	....	....
....	....	....	....
....	....	....	....

VI. MISCELLANEOUS SUPERVISORY ACTIVITIES

	Col. 1	Col. 2	Col. 3
1. Advise with student teacher as to how to secure a position	....	....	....
2. Answer inquiries from school superintendents in regard to student teacher's fitness to teach	....	....	....
3. Answer inquiries from agencies in regard to student teacher's fitness to teach	....	....	....
4. Write letters of recommendation at request of student teacher	....	....	....
5. Help student teacher to write letters of application	....	....	....
6. Advise with student teacher as to how to hold a position	....	....	....
7. Discuss with student teacher the probable differences to be found between student teaching and actual teaching	....	....	....
8. Advise with student teacher as to joining National Education Association	....	....	....
9. Advise with student teacher as to attending National Education Association meetings	....	....	....
10. Advise with student teacher as to joining state educational association	....	....	....
11. Advise with student teacher as to attending state educational association meetings	....	....	....
12. Advise with student teacher as to joining district educational association	....	....	....
13. Advise with student teacher as to attending district educational association meetings	....	....	....
14. Discuss with student teacher the need for doing professional reading ...	....	....	....
15. Advise with student teacher as to standards for choosing books for reading	....	....	....
16. Advise with student teacher as to standards for choosing magazines for reading	....	....	....
17. Advise with student teacher as to standards for choosing newspapers for reading	....	....	....
18. Advise with student teacher as to further training	....	....	....

	Col. 1	Col. 2	Col. 3

19. Advise with student teacher as to use of "visiting day" by public school teacher ....
20. Advise with student teacher concerning coöperation with fellow teachers ....
21. Advise with student teacher with regard to loyalty to school administrator ....
22. Advise with student teacher as to trips he should take during vacations .... •••• ....
23. Advise with student teacher as to how to benefit from trips taken during vacation ....
24. Review books for suitable reference materials ....
25. Review magazines for suitable reference materials ....
26. Review newspapers for suitable reference materials ....
27. Keep a record of suitable reference materials ....
28. Collect pictures for use of student teachers and children ....
29. Discuss with student teacher the value of a personal library ....
30. Write bulletins for student teachers on teaching of various subjects ....
31. Give more attention to discipline because of indirect dealing with pupils through student teacher ....
32. Supervisor constantly puts herself in place of student teacher so as to realize his difficulty ....

Please add to this list any miscellaneous supervisory activities which you know but which are not included above. Check the activities added according to instructions one, two, and three.

	Col. 1	Col. 2	Col. 3
....	....	....	....
....	....	....	....
....	....	....	....
....	....	....	••
....	....	....	....
....	....	....	....
....	....	••	....
....	....	....	....

B

SCHOOLS COÖPERATING IN THIS STUDY

State Normal School, Jacksonville, Alabama
State Teachers College, Flagstaff, Arizona
State Teachers College, Tempe, Arizona
Western State Teachers College, Gunnison, Colorado
State Normal School, Danbury, Connecticut
State Normal School, New Britain, Connecticut
State Normal School, New Haven, Connecticut
State Normal School, Albion, Idaho
State Normal School, Lewiston, Idaho
Northern Illinois State Teachers College, DeKalb, Illinois
Western Illinois State Teachers College, Macomb, Illinois
Ball State Teachers College, Muncie, Indiana
Indiana State Teachers College, Terre Haute, Indiana
Kansas State Teachers College, Pittsburg, Kansas
Western Kentucky State Teachers College, Bowling Green, Kentucky
State Normal School, Frostburg, Maryland
State Normal School, Bridgewater, Massachusetts
State Normal School, Lowell, Massachusetts
State Normal School, Salem, Massachusetts
State Normal School, Westfield, Massachusetts
Central State Teachers College, Mount Pleasant, Michigan
Michigan State Normal College, Ypsilanti, Michigan
State Teachers College, Bemidji, Minnesota
State Teachers College, St. Cloud, Minnesota
State Teachers College, Warrensburg, Missouri
State Teachers College, Kearney, Nebraska
State Normal School, Trenton, New Jersey
State Teachers College, Buffalo, New York
State Teachers College, Mayville, North Dakota
State Normal College, Bowling Green, Ohio
Southeastern State Teachers College, Durant, Oklahoma
Southwestern State Teachers College, Weatherford, Oklahoma
Southern Oregon State Normal School, Ashland, Oregon
State Teachers College, East Stroudsburg, Pennsylvania
State Teachers College, West Chester, Pennsylvania
Eastern State Normal School, Madison, South Dakota
Southern State Normal School, Springfield, South Dakota
North Texas State Teachers College, Denton, Texas
State Teachers College, East Radford, Virginia

State Teachers College, Harrisonburg, Virginia
State Normal School, Cheney, Washington
State Teachers College, Fairmont, West Virginia
State Teachers College, Eau Claire, Wisconsin
State Teachers College, Oshkosh, Wisconsin
State Teachers College, River Falls, Wisconsin

C

DECILE RANKS OF ACTIVITIES AS RATED BY 355 TRAINING SUPERVISORS

The decile ranks are numbered from 1 to 10, 1 being the lowest and 10 being the highest decile. The decile ranks for frequency of performance are indicated in Column 1, those for need for training in Column 2, and those for value to the student teacher in Column 3. The ranks are read as follows: The first activity in Section 1 is ranked in the ninth decile for frequency of performance, in the fourth decile for need for training, and in the ninth decile for value to the student teacher. The ranks for the other activities are read in the same way.

I. SUPERVISORY ACTIVITIES RELATING TO CHILDREN

	Col. 1	Col. 2	Col. 3
1. Create in children proper attitude toward student teacher	9	4	9
2. Bear responsibility for progress of children	10	5	9
3. See that pupils do not suffer from inaccuracies of student teacher	10	5	6
4. Supplement teaching of student teacher for sake of thoroughness	8	5	5
5. Direct student teacher to study habits of children	9	10	9
6. Direct student teacher to classify habits of children	4	10	3
7. Direct student teacher to study children as a group	7	10	7
8. Direct student teacher to study children as individuals	9	10	10
9. Direct student teacher to study mental characteristics of children	7	10	9
10. Direct student teacher to classify mental characteristics of children	3	10	3
11. Direct student teacher to study personal characteristics of children	7	10	9
12. Direct student teacher to classify personal characteristics of children	3	5	2
13. Direct student teacher to study interests of children	8	10	9
14. Direct student teacher to classify interests of children	3	9	3
15. Direct student teacher to study social attitudes of children	6	10	8
16. Direct student teacher to classify social attitudes of children	2	9	2
17. Direct student teacher in giving intelligence tests	1	10	3
18. Supervise student teacher in scoring intelligence tests	1	10	3
19. Supervise student teacher in tabulating results of intelligence tests	1	10	5
20. Teach student teacher to make usable records of intelligence tests results	2	10	7
21. Teach student teacher to make use of intelligence scores in planning work	3	10	6
22. Direct student teacher in giving achievement tests to children	4	10	6
23. Supervise student teacher in scoring achievement tests	4	10	5
24. Supervise student teacher in tabulating results of achievement tests	3	10	5
25. Teach student teacher to make usable records of achievement tests results	4	10	6
26. Teach student teacher to use achievement tests scores in planning work	5	10	7
27. Help student teacher to plan conference with child who has unsocial attitude	4	8	5
28. Teach student teacher to hold conference with child who has unsocial attitude	4	7	5
29. Help student teacher to plan "follow-up" conferences with child who has unsocial attitude	3	7	4
30. Teach student teacher to hold "follow-up" conferences with child who has unsocial attitude	3	7	4

	Col. 1	Col. 2	Col. 3
31. Direct student teacher to inspect children for evidences of communicable diseases	2	6	6
32. Direct student teacher to inspect children for evidences of malnutrition ..	3	9	6
33. Direct student teacher to inspect children for evidences of defective hearing	3	8	7
34. Direct student teacher to inspect children for evidences of defective vision	5	8	7
35. Direct student teacher to inspect children for evidences of defective teeth	3	8	5
36. Direct student teacher to inspect children for evidences of diseased tonsils	1	8	8
37. Direct student teacher to inspect children for evidences of adenoids	1	8	8
38. Direct student teacher to inspect children for evidences of poor posture ..	6	8	8
39. Direct student teacher to weigh children	2	4	2
40. Direct student teacher to measure heights of children	3	3	2
41. Direct student teacher to secure accurate ages of children	4	5	1
42. Direct student teacher to inspect children for evidences of nervousness ...	4	8	6
43. Teach student teacher to aid children who stutter and stammer	2	9	4
44. Teach student teacher to treat child who is left-handed	2	6	1
45. Teach student teacher to make usable records of facts relating to physical condition	3	6	3
46. Direct student teacher to make a health survey of children	1	7	3
47. Teach student teacher what teacher's responsibility for health needs of children is	6	7	7
48. Teach student teacher to take care of health needs of pupils	6	7	7
49. Direct student teacher to handle the case of the tardy child	3	3	3
50. Direct student teacher to handle the case of the habitually absent child ..	2	3	6
51. Show student teacher necessity of respecting personality of child	9	7	4
52. Teach student teacher how to respect personality of child	9	7	9
53. Require student teacher to handle disciplinary problems when he teaches	8	8	10
54. Advise with student teacher concerning disciplinary problems	10	6	10
55. See that student teacher learns that children must be happy in schoolroom	10	5	10
56. Teach student teacher how to make children happy in schoolroom	10	6	10
57. Train student teacher to check oral work of children	9	5	7
58. Teach student teacher how to grade oral work of children	7	6	6
59. Train student teacher to check written work of children	9	5	7
60. Teach student teacher how to grade written work of children	8	5	6
61. Teach student teacher how to study home life of children	3	6	4
62. Train student teacher to keep in touch with parents of children	2	3	3
63. Train student teacher to keep parents informed of progress of children ..	3	3	4
64. Teach student teacher to train children in care of all school supplies	8	2	6
65. Teach student teacher to train children in care of school furniture	8	2	5
66. Teach student teacher to train children in care of school buildings	7	2	5
67. Direct student teacher to hear reports of children on books read	5	4	2
68. Direct student teacher to hear reports of children on poems learned	4	3	2
69. Teach student teacher to provide for moral development of children	10	8	9
70. Visit homes of children with student teacher	1	2	1

II. SUPERVISORY ACTIVITIES RELATING TO STUDENT TEACHER

	Col. 1	Col. 2	Col. 3
1. Create in student teacher proper attitude toward children	9	5	9
2. Create in student proper attitude toward his work as student teacher ...	10	6	10
3. Teach student teacher to make an analysis of himself as a prospective teacher	10	6	8
4. Direct student teacher to analyze his writing from standpoint of ease of reading by children	8	4	5
5. Direct student teacher to analyze his writing from standpoint of system being taught children	7	9	7
6. Teach student teacher to be attentive to his own oral English	6	9	6
7. Teach student teacher to be attentive to his own written English	8	9	8
8. Train student teacher in habit of correcting his own oral English	9	10	10
9. Train student teacher in habit of correcting his own written English	8	10	10
10. Teach student teacher to study objectively his own achievement in school subjects	4	10	7

	Col. 1	Col. 2	Col. 3
11. Show student teacher ways of improving his knowledge of school subjects	7	9	9
12. Show student teacher necessity of constant effort to improve his knowledge of subject matter	5	8	4
13. Teach student teacher how to study	7	10	9
14. Direct student teacher in study of qualities making up best teaching personality	5	9	5
15. Advise with student teacher in matters of dress	6	9	7
16. Advise with student teacher in matters of personal cleanliness	3	8	3
17. Advise with student teacher with respect to poise of mind when standing before class	2	10	4
18. Advise with student teacher with respect to poise of body when standing before class	3	10	4
19. Direct student teacher to develop a good teaching voice	3	10	4
20. Train student teacher in ways of conserving his vitality	3	10	5
21. Stimulate and encourage student teacher	5	9	6
22. Advise with student teacher as to how to be at ease when meeting people	3	9	4
23. Advise with student teacher as to how to help others to be at ease when he is meeting them	2	9	4
24. Advise with student teacher as to how to acquire self-confidence	4	8	5
25. Advise with student teacher as to how to be tactful when dealing with parents	4	9	6
26. Advise with student teacher as to how to be tactful when dealing with children	6	9	8
27. Teach student teacher what sincerity on part of teacher involves	5	7	6
28. Teach student teacher why teacher must be judicious in choosing associates	3	6	6
29. Help student teacher to develop professional attitudes	4	8	4
30. Help student teacher to work out a professional code of ethics	3	7	4
31. Make student teacher feel at home in classroom	5	7	6
32. Respect opinions of student teacher	5	7	6
33. Have such relation to student teacher that he is always at his best when with supervisor	5	7	7
34. Create in student teacher proper attitude toward school community	5	7	7
35. Teach student teacher subject matter which he later teaches to children	2	7	4
36. Confer with student teacher who wishes help in preparation of lesson	10	5	9
37. Teach student teacher how to take notes	2	5	1
38. Require student teacher to write observation reports for all lessons observed	2	6	1
39. Require student teacher to write observation reports for some of the lessons observed	6	6	3
40. Require student teacher to write observation reports for all demonstration lessons observed	3	6	1
41. Require student teacher to write observation reports for some of the demonstration lessons observed	4	6	3
42. Give student teacher outline to guide his observations	6	8	6
43. Give student teacher questions to answer in reporting his observations	5	6	3
44. Correct observation reports	7	5	3
45. Grade observation reports before returning to student teacher	2	4	1
46. Discuss observation reports with student teacher	7	5	7
47. Check all work graded by student teacher	3	2	1
48. Frequently check work graded by student teacher	6	2	7
49. Tell student teacher of valuable references	10	7	9
50. Assign regular reference-reading to student teacher	4	5	2
51. Require student teacher to hand in notes on readings	1	2	1
52. Grade student teacher's notes on readings	1	2	1
53. Discuss with student teacher his notes on readings	2	2	1
54. Discuss with student teacher topics suggested by supervisor's study of music, art, and literature	2	5	1
55. Adjust misunderstandings which have arisen between student teacher and children	6	4	6

	Col. 1	Col. 2	Col. 3
56. Discuss with student teacher points raised by director of training in general conference	5	4	4
57. Keep a detailed record of student teacher's progress	7	7	4
58. Keep a detailed record of student teacher's needs	6	7	5
59. Require student teacher to keep a detailed record of his own progress	1	5	3
60. Require student teacher to keep a detailed record of his own needs	2	4	3
61. Put forth more effort to improve good student teacher than poor one	3	4	4
62. Put forth more effort to improve poor student teacher than good one	6	4	2
63. Rate student teacher on some rating scale	8	9	7
64. Require student teacher to rate himself on some rating scale	3	6	4
65. Compare supervisor's ratings with those of student teacher	2	3	3
66. Discuss ratings with student teacher	5	4	5
67. Show student teacher how to take objectively suggestions for improvement	7	6	9
68. Vary weekly program to care for individual differences of student teachers	5	4	3
69. Entertain student teacher at supervisor's home	1	1	1
70. Entertain student teacher elsewhere	1	1	1

III. SUPERVISORY ACTIVITIES RELATING TO TEACHING

	Col. 1	Col. 2	Col. 3
1. Teach student teacher to make lesson plans	9	10	10
2. Show student teacher relation of lesson plans to larger objectives of the school	9	10	10
3. Discuss lesson aims with student teacher	10	10	10
4. Teach student teacher to consider experiences of children in planning lessons	10	10	10
5. Teach student teacher to consider needs of children in planning lessons	10	10	10
6. Teach student teacher to consider interests of children in planning lessons	10	10	10
7. Teach student teacher to consider abilities of children in planning lessons	10	10	10
8. Teach student teacher to discover pupil-experiences appropriate for lesson to be taught	10	9	10
9. Teach student teacher to use pupil-experiences appropriate for lesson to to be taught	10	8	10
10. Direct student teacher to gather experiences from everyday life to vitalize subject matter of lesson	10	8	10
11. Teach student teacher to see that lesson provides for pupil motive	10	9	10
12. Teach student teacher to watch for original or creative work by children	9	8	8
13. Teach student teacher to keep records of original or creative work by children	3	5	3
14. Teach student teacher to discover factors influencing child to do original piece of work	4	8	5
15. Teach student teacher to analyze teaching from standpoint of plan	8	9	7
16. Correct student teacher's lesson plan	10	7	9
17. Grade student teacher's lesson plan	4	6	1
18. Discuss corrections made in lesson plan with student teacher	10	5	10
19. Provide a natural teaching situation for student teacher's first lessons	9	7	9
20. Help student teacher in planning units of work	10	9	10
21. Plan work for the student teacher to organize and work out for himself	9	7	9
22. Train student teacher to test everything he plans from standpoint of children's needs	8	8	9
23. Train student teacher to test everything he plans from standpoint of children's interests	7	7	9
24. Train student teacher to test everything he plans from standpoint of children's abilities	8	7	9
25. Show student teacher that planning is essential to good teaching	10	7	10
26. Train student teacher to get all supplementary teaching materials ready before he starts to teach the lesson	10	4	10
27. Show student teacher what preparation for teaching a lesson involves	10	8	10

	Col. 1	Col. 2	Col. 3
28. Teach demonstration lessons for student teacher	10	9	10
29. Teach student teacher to observe	9	8	10
30. Teach student teacher to interpret what is observed in terms of the laws of learning	7	10	9
31. Discuss with student teacher demonstration lessons which he has observed	8	7	8
32. Plan with student teacher term's work	6	6	5
33. Observe student teacher when he teaches	10	7	10
34. After observing student teacher, analyze his teaching procedure carefully before conferring with him	10	8	9
35. Give student teacher written criticism of his teaching	6	8	2
36. Discuss his teaching procedure with student teacher	10	7	10
37. Teach student teacher the place of pupil-activity in the lesson	10	9	10
38. Teach student teacher the place of subject matter in the lesson	10	8	10
39. Teach student teacher to recognize time and place for testing his teaching	8	8	8
40. Teach student teacher to test his teaching	9	7	9
41. Teach student teacher to use standardized tests in connection with his teaching	4	10	5
42. Teach student teacher to use informal objective tests in connection with his teaching	8	9	8
43. Direct student teacher to do the necessary "follow-up" teaching with children	9	8	10
44. Discuss with student teacher the requirements of course of study	7	6	6
45. Show student teacher that course of study is his guide and aid, not his master	8	5	8
46. Keep before student teacher the thought that subject matter is a means and not an end	9	7	9
47. Teach student teacher how to select subject matter	9	10	9
48. Teach student teacher how to organize subject matter	9	10	10
49. Give student teacher responsibility for selecting and organizing a complete unit of subject matter	8	7	8
50. Give student teacher responsibility for teaching a complete unit of subject matter	8	4	9
51. Teach student teacher to determine what parts of lesson are fundamental	9	8	10
52. Teach student teacher to determine what parts of lesson are easy for children	8	5	7
53. Teach student teacher to determine what parts of lesson are hard for children	8	5	8
54. Train student teacher to analyze his ability to direct pupil's learning activity	7	8	8
55. Teach student teacher how to determine type of learning activity to be used by pupil in mastery of any kind of subject matter	6	9	7
56. Teach student teacher to apply psychological principles with respect to individual differences	8	10	9
57. Teach student teacher to recognize time and place for different types of assignments	7	9	8
58. Teach student teacher how to make different types of assignments	7	9	9
59. Teach student teacher to determine what parts of course need different types of treatment	7	8	8
60. Show student teacher time and place for socialized classwork	8	9	7
61. Show student teacher time and place for individualized work	9	8	8
62. Show student teacher time and place for supervised study	8	8	8
63. Train student teacher to carry on socialized class work	7	9	8
64. Train student teacher to carry on individualized work	8	8	9
65. Train student teacher to carry on supervised study	8	9	9
66. Show student teacher time and place for drill work	9	8	9
67. Show student teacher time and place for problem solving	9	9	8
68. Show student teacher time and place for inductive thinking	7	9	6
69. Show student teacher time and place for deductive thinking	6	9	6

	Col. 1	Col. 2	Col. 3
70. Show student teacher time and place for project work	8	10	8
71. Show student teacher time and place for dramatization work	8	8	8
72. Show student teacher time and place for construction work by children as a means of expression of their ideas	7	9	7
73. Show student teacher time and place for creative work by children	7	9	8
74. Show student teacher time and place for appreciation lesson	9	8	8
75. Train student teacher to carry on drill work	10	8	9
76. Train student teacher to carry on problem solving	9	8	9
77. Train student teacher to carry on inductive lesson	6	9	6
78. Train student teacher to carry on deductive lesson	6	9	6
79. Train student teacher to carry on project work	8	9	9
80. Train student teacher to carry on dramatization work	7	8	7
81. Train student teacher to direct free-construction work by children	6	8	6
82. Train student teacher to direct creative work	6	8	8
83. Train student teacher to carry on appreciation lesson	8	9	8
84. Direct student teacher to study his own questioning , ...	10	8	10
85. Teach student teacher to study examples of thinking on part of children ..	6	8	8
86. Teach student teacher to discover factors influencing thinking on part of children	6	9	8
87. Teach student teacher to observe laws of learning in his teaching	8	10	9
88. Give questions to student teacher to guide his analysis of his teaching ...	5	7	6
89. Require student teacher to analyze in writing each lesson he teaches	2	4	1
90. Require student teacher to analyze in writing some of the lessons he teaches	3	4	2
91. Follow a plan of graded introduction to responsible teaching	3	6	3
92. Get student teacher to use in his teaching the methods learned in his college or normal school classes	8	5	7
93. Teach student teacher how to secure attention of children when he teaches	10	7	10
94. Hold student teacher responsible for securing attention of children when he teaches	10	4	10
95. Teach student teacher to see the good points in his teaching	10	7	10
96. Teach student teacher to see the poor points in his teaching	10	7	10
97. Teach student teacher to see why the poor points in his teaching are poor	10	8	10
98. Teach student teacher to see why the good points in his teaching are good	10	8	10
99. Train student teacher to hold children responsible for accuracy of facts ..	10	4	9
100. Hold student teacher responsible for progress of children when he teaches	10	4	10
101. Teach student teacher to test progress of children	9	6	9
102. Teach student teacher to make diagnostic records of the work of each pupil	5	9	5
103. Teach student teacher how to use diagnostic records of pupils in his teaching	5	9	5
104. Train student teacher to teach pupils to keep their own diagnostic records	3	7	3
105. Train student teacher to hold children responsible for improving their work	8	5	8
106. Hold student teacher responsible for knowing sources of his teaching information	8	6	8
107. Teach student teacher to evaluate sources of teaching information	6	7	7
108. Train student teacher to hold children responsible for knowing sources of their information	5	4	4
109. Train student teacher to teach children to evaluate sources of information	4	5	4
110. Teach student teacher to use community-life as a source for teaching materials	7	6	8
111. Teach student teacher to train children in use of textbooks	8	5	8
112. Teach student teacher to train children in use of dictionary	5	4	5
113. Teach student teacher to train children in use of reference books	6	5	6
114. Teach student teacher to train children in use of maps	5	4	6
115. Teach student teacher to train children in use of pictures	9	4	8
116. Teach student teacher to train children in use of card catalog	1	5	2
117. Teach student teacher to train children in use of magazines	5	3	5
118. Teach student teacher to train children in use of newspapers	4	4	5
119. Teach student teacher use of blackboard in class	9	4	8
120. Teach student teacher use of bulletin board	8	3	5

	Col. 1	Col. 2	Col. 3
121. Teach student teacher use of lantern and slides	2	6	2
122. Teach student teacher to use visual aids in his teaching	8	6	7
123. Teach student teacher to use verbal illustration in his teaching	8	5	7
124. Teach student teacher to distinguish between method and device	7	8	7
125. Teach student teacher to train children to make a notebook	4	3	2
126. Teach student teacher to train children in use of notebook	4	3	2
127. Direct student teacher to other classrooms to see outstanding pieces of work	4	5	4
128. Teach student teacher to correlate different school subjects	9	7	9
129. Teach student teacher to correlate handwork or construction work with subject matter lessons	8	7	7
130. Direct student teacher to sources of good supplementary teaching materials	9	6	9
131. Teach student teacher to plan school excursion	3	5	3
132. Teach student teacher to visit institutions and places of business to make arrangements for school excursion	2	3	2
133. Teach student teacher to carry out plans for school excursion	2	3	3
134. Teach student teacher to plan opening exercises	6	3	4
135. Teach student teacher to take charge of opening exercises	7	3	4
136. Help student teacher to build up a teaching technique based on psychological principles	8	10	10
137. Direct student teacher to start collecting good teaching materials........	9	5	10
138. Direct student teacher to start collecting teaching methods used by good teachers	7	5	8

IV.   SUPERVISORY ACTIVITIES RELATING TO SCHOOL AND CLASSROOM MANAGEMENT

	Col. 1	Col. 2	Col. 3
1. Teach student teacher to care for lighting of classroom	9	6	9
2. Teach student teacher to care for ventilation of classroom	9	6	9
3. Teach student teacher to care for temperature of classroom	8	6	9
4. Teach student teacher to check the seating of children	8	4	7
5. Require student teacher to adjust seats for children	3	4	5
6. Teach student teacher proper placement of all school furniture	5	5	4
7. Teach student teacher to see the principles guiding proper placement of school furniture	5	6	5
8. Teach student teacher to see the principles for caring for physical conditions of classroom	7	7	8
9. Teach student teacher standards as to permanent schoolroom decoration	5	6	4
10. Teach student teacher standards as to temporary schoolroom decoration	6	5	4
11. Teach student teacher to supervise children in decorating classroom for special days	5	3	2
12. Teach student teacher to supervise children in decorating classroom for special weeks	4	3	1
13. Teach student teacher to supervise children in decorating classroom for school parties	3	2	1
14. Teach student teacher to help children plan program for special days	4	3	2
15. Teach student teacher to help children plan program for special weeks ...	4	2	3
16. Teach student teacher to help children plan program for school parties ...	4	3	2
17. Teach student teacher to help children carry out plans for special days ...	5	3	1
18. Teach student teacher to help children carry out program for special weeks	4	3	5
19. Teach student teacher to help children carry out program for school parties	3	2	2
20. Teach student teacher to supervise children's preparation for school programs	5	3	3
21. Train student teacher to direct making of costumes for various occasions .	2	3	1
22. Train student teacher to do teacher's part in keeping classroom clean	9	2	7
23. Train student teacher to do teacher's part in keeping school building and yard clean	5	2	4
24. Teach student teacher to train children to be considerate of janitor	6	1	6

	Col. 1	Col. 2	Col. 3
25. Teach student teacher to train children in keeping classroom clean	9	2	8
26. Teach student teacher to train children in keeping school building and yard clean	6	1	7
27. Create in student teacher proper attitude toward school janitor	6	1	5
28. Advise with student teacher as to what things a teacher may expect a janitor to do	3	2	2
29. Teach student teacher to inspect toilets	1	2	1
30. Teach student teacher to inspect wardrobes	2	1	2
31. Teach student teacher to inspect children's desks	5	1	3
32. Teach student teacher to inspect children's lockers	1	1	2
33. Require student teacher to report inspections in writing	1	1	1
34. Require student teacher to report inspections orally	2	1	2
35. Discuss with student teacher the report of his inspections	2	2	2
36. Teach student teacher proper procedure if inspections show unfavorable conditions	3	2	2
37. Direct student teacher to wash blackboards	3	1	1
38. Direct student teacher to clean erasers	2	1	1
39. Direct student teacher to wash windows	1	1	1
40. Teach student teacher to supervise washing of windows by children	1	1	1
41. Teach student teacher to supervise washing of blackboards by children ..	1	1	1
42. Teach student teacher to supervise cleaning of erasers by children	1	1	1
43. Teach student teacher to supervise children at indoor play	7	6	7
44. Teach student teacher to supervise children at play on playground	6	6	7
45. Teach student teacher to supervise children going to toilet	6	2	3
46. Teach student teacher to supervise children getting a drink	5	1	2
47. Teach student teacher to train children as to time for leaving room	6	1	3
48. Train student teacher to routinize caring for children's wraps	5	1	3
49. Train student teacher to routinize passing of lines	7	1	3
50. Train student teacher to do hall duty	5	1	2
51. Teach student teacher to supervise children sharpening pencils	3	1	1
52. Teach student teacher to keep daily register	5	3	5
53. Teach student teacher to keep daily grades of children's work	6	3	5
54. Teach student teacher to keep test grades of children's work	7	3	6
55. Train student teacher to record children's grades in teacher's record book	5	2	3
56. Train student teacher to fill out children's report book or card	3	2	3
57. Give student teacher practice in handling office records	1	3	1
58. Check all clerical work done by student teacher	4	1	2
59. Train student teacher to take charge of fire drills	1	2	2
60. Train student teacher to give first-aid in case of illness	2	7	5
61. Train student teacher to give first-aid in case of accidents	2	6	5
62. Discuss with student teacher the making of daily program	5	5	7
63. Hold student teacher responsible for meeting and dismissing classes on time	9	1	8
64. Train student teacher to supervise children's library period	6	4	5
65. Train student teacher to supervise children's story hour	4	4	4
66. Discuss with student teacher value of parent-teachers' association	2	4	2
67. Show student teacher teacher's responsibility with respect to parent-teachers' association	1	3	2
68. Give student teacher opportunity to participate in parent-teachers' association	1	2	1
69. Give student teacher opportunity to assist with school teas for parents ...	1	2	1
70. Train student teacher to supplement children's lunch with a hot dish	1	2	1
71. Discuss with student teacher values of some form of pupil self-government	5	6	5
72. Direct student teacher to study pupil self-government of the classroom ..	5	5	4
73. Direct student teacher to study pupil self-government of the school	2	5	3
74. Give student teacher opportunity to observe the meetings of school council	1	2	1
75. Train student teacher to supervise pupil monitors in the classroom	4	2	2
76. Show student teacher how to supervise pupil-selection of pupil monitors ..	3	2	2
77. Train student teacher to supervise pupil-assignment of duties to pupil monitors	2	1	2

V.   SUPERVISORY ACTIVITIES RELATING TO ADMINISTRATION OF STUDENT
TEACHING PROGRAM

	Col. 1	Col. 2	Col. 3
1. Attend meetings of supervisors called by director of training	9	1	6
2. Note problems which occur in supervising student teaching	9	6	8
3. Report to director of training problems to be discussed at meetings of training supervisors	4	2	4
4. Attend general conferences of student teachers conducted by director of training	2	1	4
5. Note problems occurring in supervising student teaching which should be taken up in general conferences with student teachers by director of training	4	4	5
6. Report problems to director of training to be discussed at general conferences with student teachers	3	2	5
7. Note points made by director of training at conferences to discuss with student teachers	6	2	6
8. Confer with director of training concerning student teacher whom he has visited	7	2	7
9. Confer with director of training with respect to problems of supervision of student teachers	7	3	7
10. Report to director of training student teacher whose work is below standard	9	2	7
11. Report to director of training student teacher whose work is above standard	7	2	6
12. Report to director of training analysis of reasons for successes of student teachers	6	6	5
13. Report to director of training analysis of reasons for failures of student teachers	7	6	6
14. Report to director of training analysis of the progress of each student teacher each month	2	3	2
15. Report to director of training at end of term detailed statement of student teacher's fitness to teach	9	4	7
16. Grade the teaching of student teacher at end of term	10	5	6
17. Report term grade of student teacher to director of training	9	1	6
18. Report term grade of student teacher to registrar	2	1	1
19. Adjust daily program for director of training to fit student teaching assignments	6	1	3
20. Select student teacher's best lesson plan for filing with director of training	1	2	1
21. Hold individual conferences with student teacher each day	6	6	5
22. Hold individual conferences with student teacher each week	9	6	7
23. Hold group conferences each week with student teachers	6	7	6
24. Hold student teacher responsible for preparing for group conferences	3	3	2
25. Assign topics to student teacher for conference discussion	3	5	2
26. Confer with members of college or normal school faculty as to most helpful prerequisite courses for student teachers	1	5	4
27. Confer with members of college or normal school faculty as to strong points in student teacher's training	2	4	4
28. Confer with members of college or normal school faculty as to weak points in student teacher's training	2	4	4
29. Confer with subject matter teachers in college or normal school with reference to teaching materials for student teacher	1	4	4
30. Confer with teachers of educational theory in college or normal school with regard to principles of teaching for student teacher	1	5	5
31. Invite members of college or normal school faculty to visit training supervisor's classes	2	1	3
32. Confer with members of college or normal school faculty who have visited supervisor's classes with respect to the teaching	2	2	4
33. Confer with members of college or normal school faculty who have visited supervisor's classes with respect to subject matter being used	2	2	3
34. Visit classes taught by members of college or normal school faculty	1	1	2
35. Confer with members of college or normal school faculty with regard to their courses	1	3	3

VI. MISCELLANEOUS SUPERVISORY ACTIVITIES

	Col. 1	Col. 2	Col. 3
1. Advise with student teacher as to how to secure a position	4	4	3
2. Answer inquiries from school superintendents in regard to student teacher's fitness to teach	4	3	3
3. Answer inquiries from agencies in regard to student teacher's fitness to teach	4	2	3
4. Write letters of recommendation at request of student teacher	4	3	3
5. Help student teacher to write letters of application	2	3	2
6. Advise with student teacher as to how to hold a position	4	3	5
7. Discuss with student teacher the probable differences to be found between student teaching and actual teaching	7	4	7
8. Advise with student teacher as to joining National Education Association	1	1	1
9. Advise with student teacher as to attending National Education Association meetings	1	1	1
10. Advise with student teacher as to joining state educational association ...	1	1	2
11. Advise with student teacher as to attending state educational association meetings	1	1	1
12. Advise with student teacher as to joining district educational association .	8	1	2
13. Advise with student teacher as to attending district educational association meetings	1	1	2
14. Discuss with student teacher the need for doing professional reading	7	3	8
15. Advise with student teacher as to standards for choosing books for reading	4	5	6
16. Advise with student teacher as to standards for choosing magazines for reading	4	5	6
17. Advise with student teacher as to standards for choosing newspapers for reading	2	4	4
18. Advise with student teacher as to further training	5	3	6
19. Advise with student teacher as to use of "visiting day" by public school teacher	2	2	2
20. Advise with student teacher concerning coöperation with fellow teachers	6	2	8
21. Advise with student teacher with regard to loyalty to school administrator	7	2	8
22. Advise with student teacher as to trips he should take during vacations ..	1	2	1
23. Advise with student teacher as to how to benefit from trips taken during vacation	1	2	1
24. Review books for suitable reference materials	5	5	4
25. Review magazines for suitable reference materials	5	6	6
26. Review newspapers for suitable reference materials	4	3	3
27. Keep a record of suitable reference materials	6	4	7
28. Collect pictures for use of student teachers and children	9	2	6
29. Discuss with student teacher the value of a personal library	5	2	5
30. Write bulletins for student teachers on teaching of various subjects	1	4	1
31. Give more attention to discipline because of indirect dealing with pupils through student teacher	7	3	4
32. Supervisor constantly puts herself in place of student teacher so as to realize his difficulty	9	3	9

D

STATEMENTS OF EXPERIENCES IN STUDENT TEACHING BY STUDENT TEACHERS

This statement was submitted by a student teacher who had completed thirty-six weeks of student teaching.

I. Things my critics did for me, or provided opportunities for me to do, which helped me:

1. My critics have given me much responsibility.
2. They have given me lists of sources of materials to enrich my knowledge and to enable me to plan better lesson procedures.
3. They gave me an opportunity to teach an observation lesson.
4. They have given me encouragement and a desire to become a good teacher.
5. They gave me a chance to help in decorating the classroom.
6. They gave me their ideas and a clear understanding of the work to be done.
7. They have shown a real appreciation of my efforts.

II. Things I wanted my critics to do for me, or to provide opportunities for me to do, which were not done:

1. My critics did everything for me that they could. They will always stand out in my mind as people who believed in me and I hope to justify their belief and never disappoint them.
2. If student teachers could have an opportunity to teach music or art (things in which they have not majored) I think it would be beneficial. It is unfortunate that student teachers get experience in only three or four subjects. If we were allowed to spend a longer time each day in the training school we could have a chance to use a wider variety of material and of subject matter. We need to have contact with more than we are able to have with our period of teaching as it is now.

A second student who had completed twenty-four weeks of work as a student teacher submitted this statement:

I. Things my critics did for me, or provided opportunities for me to do, which helped me:

1. Helped me in lesson planning.
2. Showed me different types of lessons and discussed with me ways of teaching them.
3. Helped me with my own writing and printing.
4. Helped me improve my voice and manner.
5. Helped me with discipline problems.
6. Gave me some idea as to grading, making term grades, keeping records, making reports, and talking to agents.

7. Permitted me to handle the sand-table work.
8. Showed me what a great part personality plays in our school work.
9. Gave me ideas as to flash cards both in numbers and reading.
10. Showed me how to use flash cards.
11. Gave me ideas as to seating, lighting, and ventilation.
12. Showed me the importance of story telling.
13. Showed me how to help children overcome pointing and lip movement.
14. Gave me chance to take charge of the toy orchestra.
15. Gave me opportunities to give and direct seat work.
16. Showed me the value of using different textbooks in primary reading.
17. Helped me to see and use chances for character building.
18. Taught me to use the mimeograph.
19. Gave me the opportunity to watch the school nurse examine the children.
20. Helped me to see what a great part the child's attendance plays in his school work.
21. Let me help weigh and measure the children.
22. Helped me to see what a great part home environment plays in the child's life and school work.
23. Gave me the opportunity of helping take the children to the play at the Masonic Temple. I learned what a great problem this will be when I take my children on an excursion.
24. Helped me to see value of the tables and chairs as compared with the school desk.
25. Gave me the opportunity to take charge of the whole room and feel the responsibility of teaching.

11. Things I wanted my critics to do for me, or provide opportunity for me to do, which were not done:

1. I did not get so much work in dramatization as I should have liked. I wish we might have had more time each day for student teaching than we have had and carry fewer other subjects.

This third statement was submitted by a student teacher who had completed twenty weeks of student teaching. The statement follows:

I. Things my critics did for me, or provided opportunities for me to do, which helped me:

1. My critic teachers have really taught me the technique of teaching. They have given me opportunity to show my skill in managing a classroom and in carrying out my own units of work. With the aid of suggestions from the critics the units have been worked out successfully and have been proved to be of great interest to children. I have had the opportunity to carry out a sand-table project in connection with a social studies unit. My critics have showed me also how to plan and take an excursion.
2. One day we had a new rote song to teach to the children. The time was rather hard to learn and the children did not seem to be able to get it. The critic took the lesson and showed me just

how to get the children to listen carefully to learn the time. I am very glad to have had this help. The lessons that I have observed and the opportunities I have had to teach have proved very valuable to me. This has been particularly true in phonics.

II. Things I wanted my critics to do for me, or to provide opportunities for me to do, which were not done:

1. One critic teacher would not allow me to teach a new rote song the way we were taught at the normal school. She also made me change the specific purposes of my lesson plan to conform to her own. They had to be written just so, and written in her own words. The social studies work taught by this critic was pasting and arranging pictures steadily for two weeks. The reading lessons were monotonous for the children. The same story was read three times. The criticisms given me by this teacher never had anything to do with the lessons I taught. Many things around the room (for example, washing the blackboards) had to be done again and again before they were done satisfactorily, not looking any better than they had the first time. Another critic, when she taught social studies or nature study, told the story to the children and then had them relate the story back to her. She was able to hold the attention of the children by the way she told the story. In spite of these criticisms I can really say that my training has been very valuable to me and will certainly aid me in conducting a class of my own.

A fourth statement was submitted by a student teacher who had completed forty weeks of experience in student teaching. The statement follows:

I. Things my critics did for me, or provided opportunities for me to do, which helped me:

1. Gave valuable suggestions in regard to voice control.
2. Showed me how to use lantern and slides.
3. Showed me how to use the mimeograph.
4. Gave me copies of stories and poems they considered valuable and told me where to find others.

II. Things I wanted my critics to do for me, or to provide opportunities for me to do, which were not done:

1. Except in my last term of teaching, I received no personal criticism. I have never seen my rating card and so I never knew the points on which I was being marked. The fact that I never raised my teaching mark I partly lay to the fact that I was never told just what I should be working on most. When I was teaching in the first grade the only thing that was told me every day until about one week before the end of the term was that everything was going fine, that my work was splendid. Still I received only a "C" mark.

The fifth statement was submitted by a student teacher who had completed sixteen weeks of work in student teaching. The statement follows:

1. Things my critics did for me, or provided opportunities for me to do, which helped me:

1. Helped me to acquire an understanding of child nature and knowledge as to how to treat children.
2. Gave me help in certain shortcomings; for example, art.
3. Permitted me to work out the principles learned in the normal school.
4. Told me of sources of valuable teaching materials.
5. Coöperated in any projects or units which I took up.
6. Helped me to learn what to expect of children and what to demand.
7. Helped me in wording questions which will bring the best results.
8. Called my attention to minor points which very often count in the schoolroom.
9. Permitted me to do much independent teaching at the last.

II. Things I wanted my critics to do for me, or to provide opportunities for me to do, which were not done:

1. I wanted less unnecessary and routine criticism and more actual help.
2. I wanted more face-to-face talks about personal and school matters.
3. I wanted more consideration as far as menial tasks are concerned. We are not in the army.
4. I wanted more actual teaching when first starting out. I found observation of little or no help.
5. I wanted to teach more nature study and hygiene in the lower grades.
6. I expected a friendlier attitude on the part of the critics.
7. I expected less feeling of competition on the part of student teachers working with the same critic and more coöperation and good sportsmanship.
8. I do not think a student teacher should have to teach before several supervisors at one time until the very end of the term. It is nerve-racking. Even the critic becomes flustered before such a group.
9. I did not expect the critic teacher would let personal feeling enter into final reports to supervisors.

E

SUPERVISORY TECHNIQUES

I. Techniques Reported by Group I

The important opportunity awaiting the student teacher is:

1. "To have practical experience in dealing with children. The student is given his own group of children. I take up with him the plan of the work and after 2 or 3 weeks he assumes responsibility for all work of his group."

2. "Actually teaching under close supervision. The work begins with observation of my teaching of subjects, the method of teaching of which can be most easily imitated. The teaching method can be seen most easily in spelling. In connection with this observation of spelling I ask the student to read the chapter in Parker's *Types of Elementary Teaching and Learning* which deals with the teaching of spelling. I also start the work in reading rather early. I divide the children into ability groups for reading. After some directed observation the student takes charge of the reading work of one group."

3. "To be able to work with the children with guidance of a supervisor who is concerned about the welfare of the children and the growth of the student as a teacher; and to have his first teaching in a subject in the teaching of which he can see the results of his efforts. I am able generally to help a student teacher to secure most easily results which he can see in the teaching of writing. Seeing results of his teaching makes the student feel that he is a teacher."

4. "To try out with the children the theories and principles learned in the college classes. Each student teacher plans his own program. He must provide for the requirements of the course of study. Aside from that he is free to do his work as he likes."

5. "To learn to help children to make the most of themselves. In doing this he will have the opportunity to answer in actual teaching situations all the questions which his work in the college has given him."

6. "To learn how to promote desirable changes in pupils through the use of subject matter. This is done through a study of the playground activities which afford many illustrations of self-directed pupil leadership, pupil organization, and pupil selection of games; through participation in the health work which stimulates in the boys and girls health ideals; and through sharing with me the work of the classroom which provides opportunity for the boys and girls to acquire skills, information, attitudes, and ideals."

7. "To be able to study teaching; to be able to concentrate on the purpose of the lesson so as not to be side-tracked by what children say during the progress of the lesson."

8. "To assume responsibility; to feel himself a part of things; to come to have a notion of what the teaching task is; to have the opportunity to work with a group of children who are trying to learn to direct their own thinking, planning, and work; and to come to have a sympathetic and co-operative feeling toward such children. I ask the student to try to forget me. I have been as he is and I know how he feels. I tell him to be himself and to let the children be themselves; I ask him to try to discover his points of strength and of weakness. After some observation and par-ticipation I ask him to write a rather complete statement of what he thinks he can do and what he thinks he cannot do; of what characteristics of manner and voice he feels he needs to try to acquire. Our problem then becomes, How go about acquiring these things which he lacks?"

9. "To work on an equal basis with an experienced teacher; to come to feel at home with a group of children and to be happy while working with them. I find out what he can do successfully and then plan work for him to do so that his initial teaching efforts will be successful."

10. "To learn to work with children."

11. "To do actual teaching, preceded by carefully directed observation so that he may come to see what being adequately prepared to teach involves; to have conferences with a supervisor for the purpose of working out the psychological principles underlying the teaching techniques used."

12. "To acquire the necessary teaching personality—poise, tact, dignity—to meet any classroom situation. The student can improve his knowledge of subject matter and of method by himself if he is intelligent and indus-trious. To put emphasis upon subject matter causes the student to lose sight of the teaching personality side."

13. "Learning to plan his work, to be resourceful in assembling and organizing subject matter so that it may be presented to children in concise sequence; learning to evaluate teaching materials and his ability to teach."

14. "To observe the teaching of the supervisor who directs his attention to anticipated difficulties and to the plans which have been made to meet these difficulties. Conferences always follow the demonstration teaching in which the successes and failures of the procedures planned to meet antici-pated difficulties are discussed. The aim is to insure first teaching attempts being successful."

15. "To learn as a teacher to be humanly interested in the children and in the work the children are doing. I give specific directions to the student so that he may acquire early this interest and then show him by directing his observation of my teaching, how this interest in children and in the work of children is an essential teaching quality."

16. "To have the responsibility of teaching and controlling children; to have things to do which are essential to the work of the classroom and which prepare him for teaching; to teach children in a room by himself so that he may feel that the task is his; and to be held constantly for a high degree of attainment."

17. "To develop teaching personality—a pleasing voice, cheerful aggres-siveness, the manner of teaching as if he likes to teach, and qualities of

leadership. I frankly point out to him things in his own conduct, dress, manner, and teaching procedure which he needs to improve."

Lesson planning:

1. "I ask the student teacher to make unit lesson plans for blocks of subject matter, but daily lesson plans for the seat work following the class period."

2. "Every student teacher hands in detailed lesson plans of all lessons he teaches during the first part of the term. Unit plans are used for a series of lessons in the same unit of subject matter. I always teach such lessons as will lead directly up to the work which the student is planning. My aim in doing this is to insure that the children will have a proper basis for the work which the student will teach. I want him to use his own ideas in planning. As the term progresses and as the student improves in planning and in teaching, less detailed plans are required. I ask that the plan include the subject matter and procedure, and the important questions which the student teacher plans to ask."

3. "The student teachers are taught lesson planning in the normal school. I find out what they can do with planning by asking them to write a plan for the lesson which they hear me assign to the pupils. Then we discuss this plan in a conference. I find it hard to help the student teacher to see the value of the pupil's aim. I regard the introduction as very valuable if the plan is for the first lesson in a series dealing with the same unit of subject matter. I ask the student to observe my teaching of the first lesson in a series dealing with the same unit of subject matter. We hold a conference in which we discuss the use of this part of the plan. Then the student writes his plan. We also have trouble with the conclusion or summary. Here again demonstration and conference are used. Planning at the end of the term is much less detailed than at the beginning. No planning in spelling is required. In the beginning I ask the student to indicate in writing the spelling method we are using so that I may be sure he understands it. The form of the plan we use covers the teacher's and pupil's aims, a statement of the materials and procedure to be used, the introduction—if the lesson is the first one in a series—an outline of the lesson, and a summary or conclusion."

4. "I do not have the student teacher write lesson plans as such. It takes the time which the student needs to spend on his preparation for his work with the children. In this grade (second) the work in reading and language is fundamental. I direct the student teacher to study carefully the way I handle the work. I ask him to indicate on paper all suggestions he has to make for teaching reading and language as the result of his course in college and which his observation of my teaching causes him to think he can use when he teaches. This enables me to help the student teacher use what he has learned in the college and keeps me more up to date also. Then I let him teach using these suggestions he has learned in the college. I do have the student write out the important test questions which he plans to ask the children."

5. "In the beginning I plan everything and I tell the student just what

to do. As soon as he is able I permit him to do everything for himself. We use no written plans as such. We use plans of units of work in which the aims to be attained are set up and the sequence of subject matter necessary to attain the aims is outlined. Formal lesson planning allows no place for the child's reactions."

6. "I direct the student teacher to observe my teaching. I tell the student the steps in the lesson as I think of them. They are aims, arousing pupils' interest, the instruction, and testing the instruction. The student writes a report of the lesson to show that he sees the four steps of the lesson. At first his reports are a reproduction of what happens. As soon as he is able to see everything which happens we start analyzing the teaching with a view to seeing the underlying psychological principles."

7. "At first I have little real lesson planning. I want the student to learn to talk and work with the children. I tell the student just what to do. I set the purpose for the early lessons which the student teaches, following the pattern of the demonstration lesson which has preceded. After he begins to have some conception of what teaching is I have him select and organize the teaching materials for the lessons and to write rather full plans. His chief concern at this stage is questioning. As soon as possible we change the plan from the daily to the unit type. In this grade (first) the seat work is very important. I find it very difficult to help the student to plan seat work which provides educative experiences for the children."

8. "I ask the student to observe my teaching of a lesson and to report the lesson in plan form. In conference we take up all questions which the student wants to raise. If all points of the plan have not been discussed I raise other questions, trying to impress upon the student that there are other ways of teaching such a lesson. I often raise the question, How would you plan to take care of this point? I do not want the student to merely imitate me when he teaches. Then I give the student a definite assignment to teach and ask him to prepare a detailed plan of the lesson. The plan is to be handed to me two days before the lesson is to be taught to permit making needed revisions. For a time I require the student to prepare detailed lesson plans for all lessons he teaches. Later less detailed plans are required and the student is directed to spend his time studying the plans of the other student teachers. I encourage the student teachers to confer with one another and to study one another's plans."

9. "I permit the student teacher to make the type of plan he wants to make. The only requirement is that the plan be his best preparation to teach. I have found that formal plans prevent the teacher from teaching the children. Informal planning helps to cultivate a desirable teacher-pupil relationship. I ask him to indicate in his plan enough to make clear what he plans to do. We use unit plans rather than daily plans. The daily connections are indicated in the unit plan by means of a colored pencil."

10. "I provide the student teacher with a model lesson plan—one of my own or one of a former student teacher. We discuss all the points in the plan, trying to see how the form of plan for a certain lesson in one subject applies to all lessons in all subjects. Following this conference, the student observes me teach with a view to seeing if he can pick out the parts of

the plan. As soon as the student is able to understand the plan and to see that it is essential to good teaching we take up unit planning. Most of our planning is of the unit type."

11. "I give the student the plans for all lessons which I ask him specifically to observe. This permits him to follow each step of the lesson as the teaching proceeds. I ask him to make notes of all points which he wants to discuss in conference. At first he has few points to discuss. I then put questions to him. We continue this until he is able to discuss the lesson observed from the standpoint of the plan and to raise questions. I cover each type of lesson in this way—drill, information, problem-solving, and appreciation. Then the student may refer to these plans when he teaches. I urge him to use his own ideas when he plans and not copy only."

12. "I start the work in lesson planning by having the student teacher write observation reports of the lesson which he sees me teach. After he has learned to write a satisfactory observation report I give him instruction for plan writing. The plan includes aims, content, materials needed, procedure, introduction, questions, possible pupil responses, and the accomplishment check. The accomplishment check is to discover who learned and who did not. After the student teacher becomes able to write good plans according to this form we take up the unit plan which has four divisions— aims, teacher activities, pupil activities, and accomplishment check. At first the unit plan is made out in detail. Toward the end of the term, if the student is doing good teaching, the unit plans are less detailed."

13. "I have the student teacher write in plan form an observation report of my teaching. I tell him that in planning my lessons I think through the aims, procedure, and ways of testing results and ask him to try to see these steps in my teaching. We discuss this observation report in our conference and clear up all the student's difficulties. The next day he brings in the completed plan. After he has come to see the relation of planning to teaching and has learned to prepare good plans I assign some teaching to him for which daily plans are required. After a fair degree of skill in teaching and in making daily lesson plans is attained I give the student the responsibility for organizing and teaching a complete unit of work for which a unit plan is made. If he teaches well, later unit plans are less detailed but I tend to favor detailed plans. It insures making careful preparation. I ask the student teacher to test his teaching at the close of each lesson and also at the close of a unit of work. The unit plan covers the same steps as the daily lesson plan."

14. "The student teacher and I plan a small unit of work together which I teach. Then I teach lessons which I have planned by myself and which he is to observe and report in plan form. We follow this with his planning lessons which he is to teach. These first plans are detailed and I check them closely before the student teaches the lesson. I want to be sure that the plan has provided for the interests and needs of the children. In the last part of the teaching I give less supervision to the planning and the plans are less detailed. I always check them to see that the procedure planned will insure the aims being accomplished."

15. "I give the student teacher an outline on lesson planning and ask him

to prepare a lesson following the outline. I ask him to make the plan sufficiently detailed to show he knows the necessary subject matter. . . . As soon as he becomes skilled in making the daily lesson plan we change to the unit plan. I want the student to use his own ideas and not to imitate me."

16. "I let the student teacher know what the requirements of the course of study are. He knows then what we have to do and how much time we have for doing it. I ask him to separate the work to be done into units and try to find out how many lessons are needed to cover the required work. I require rather definite planning covering teacher and pupil aims, introduction or point of contact with earlier work, procedure, and conclusion or summary. I ask the student to be rather definite in the procedure. The plans are rather complete in the beginning. Later we spend less time on detailed plans and more time on organization of teaching materials."

17. "I ask the student to bring in his idea of a plan. This gives us a basis for a conference on lesson planning. Our final plan covers aims, approach, subject matter, check. I ask for daily plans throughout the term although they are not so detailed at the last."

Selection and organization of teaching materials:

1. "The collecting of teaching materials is a hard problem. I show the student teacher what former student teachers have done. One former student teacher planned and carried out a dairy farm project, the interest in which was developed by a visit to a neighboring dairy farm. This project as planned by the children under the guidance of the teacher involved making a school garden, number work, reading work, language work—both oral and written—and entertaining the children of the second grade in order that they might use up the butter which they had made as the result of following one line of interest. A second student teacher planned an Indian project which culminated in an entertainment of the parents. To carry out the project the children had many reading, language—both oral and written—art, music, and dramatization lessons. The student teachers got a great deal of experience in selecting and organizing teaching materials in carrying out their projects."

2. "It is hard to get the students to do much with this. They are willing to depend upon the textbooks. I ask them to gather pictures, stories, and poems to supplement the materials of the textbooks."

3. "That is one of the hardest things. I have a wealth of material dealing with Greek and Roman history. I ask the students to become familiar with it. I am afraid I do not succeed in getting them to collect much teaching material."

4. "I do this best by means of project work. One student teacher planned a milk project. This involved the study of the production and shipping of milk, and handling it until it reaches the home where it is used. Emphasis was placed upon the precautions taken to keep it clean and reasons why these precautions are taken. The student teacher was successful in creating a genuine interest in the children and they, with his guidance, collected a large part of the materials needed. Student teachers gather a great deal

of supplementary reading material dealing with such topics as children in other lands and health."

5. "I show the student teacher what teaching materials I have collected and we use these materials a great deal through the term. I suggest to the student sources for such materials and show him different ways of filing them so that they are available for use. I emphasize the necessity of having teaching materials organized and filed so that they may be used readily."

6. "I urge the student to bring in supplementary materials for every lesson. We use the city and normal school libraries and take several excursions in order to find supplementary materials."

7. "I suggest sources for supplementary teaching materials and the student does bring in some. I am afraid I do not do much with this, however."

8. "I show the student teacher that things which the children say and questions which they ask are really leads to valuable supplementary teaching materials. I ask the children to bring to school good examples of description, pieces of poetry, and other types of selections which have interested them. I suggest to the student teacher how he can see work ahead so as to have time to collect pictures and other supplementary materials."

9. "I have a classified collection of teaching materials which I have been gathering for many years. I show this to the student teacher and tell him how I have collected it. I suggest to him to do the same thing. We make a great deal of use of my collection so he sees its value. I ask the children to bring in materials which they find outside of school which interest them. Much of this is valuable material and I add it to my collection in case the children do not wish to keep it. I try to help the student to acquire standards for judging such material so that he may know what to keep and what to throw away. We take many excursions. The student teacher goes first and selects the places which we shall visit. The things which we see and find and bring back to school with us serve as a basis for many oral and written language, geography, and history lessons. The student learns that the excursion needs careful planning and handling if it is to provide educative experiences for the children."

10. "I have lists of sources from which valuable teaching materials may be obtained. I ask the students to copy these lists. I have pictures and clippings, exhibits of cotton and wool, and other illustrative material all catalogued. I ask the students to collect as much as they can while in training. I also have many books treating principles of teaching, case studies of problem children, and other problems, which the student teachers use freely."

11. "I have lists of reference books which have proved valuable and lists of sources from which teaching materials may be obtained. The students copy these lists. To insure that they see that these lists can be used I plan work for each student which necessitates his getting at least one rather valuable piece of material from one of these sources. The student thus sees how valuable these lists are. In planning a unit of work I direct the students to bring in all the supplementary materials they can find. In conferences we evaluate this material and plan the use of what is suitable for the children. I emphasize the point that a teacher must know much more than he teaches."

12. "I try first to show the student that I am more than a textbook teacher. I have my own materials at hand—books, magazines, pictures, clippings, and exhibits. I have these catalogued and filed so that I can find just what I want when I need it. Then, too, I know the homes from which my children come so well that we are able to secure much valuable material through the children. The public library has a great deal of material—books and pictures—which the student teachers use."

13. "I have a great deal of material catalogued and filed which the student teachers and I used constantly in our work with the children.[1] I help the student teacher to see how a wealth of supplementary teaching materials carefully organized facilitates correlation of all school work. In connection with our reading of Eskimo stories we plan to take up the Eskimos in our work in language, music, art, and industrial arts."

14. "I ask the student teacher to watch the local papers for items which will be of interest and value. We also have the children write letters to factories asking for sample materials. We find many valuable materials in the homes which the children bring."

15. "The student teacher asks the children to bring in materials, such as pictures, stories, poems, and objects, which relate to their work at school and which interest them. We use the school excursion a great deal. The student teacher plans and makes the arrangements and carries out the plans. I have a great deal of historical and geographical material which the student teachers use."

16. "It is difficult to get the student to be resourceful in gathering teaching materials. We ask the children to bring in materials. Our training school library, our normal school library, and our public library have a great deal of material which is available for our use. I ask each student teacher to become familiar with what is in each one so that when occasion demands he knows where to secure supplementary materials. I have one student teacher this term who takes his children on a nature trip each Saturday morning. He is securing good materials which he uses in his teaching the following week."

17. "Our aim is to help our children use many sources as helps in their study. Our room library, our training school library, and our normal school library have a great deal of valuable material which can be used by the children. I ask the student teacher to see what is available in all three libraries and to prepare a list of the materials which he can use. The student teacher takes his children on excursions and nature trips. I am afraid that I tend to make the plans for all of these trips."

Analysis of teaching and of teaching personality by the student teacher:

1. "We have a rating form which does not satisfy us. The students are acquainted with the points of the form when they come to their teaching.

[1] This supervisor's card catalog showed that she had gathered a great deal of material —stories, pictures, and clippings—relating to a large variety of topics in which children are interested. Some of these topics were: Arbor Day, Armistice Day, birds, Boys' Week, bugs, butterflies, children of other lands, Christmas, clocks, cotton, fires and fire-prevention, flags, Franklin, great visitors, how people travel, Indians, insects, Lincoln, Memorial Day, Red Cross, thrift, trees, Roosevelt, Washington.

I discuss each point carefully with the student at the middle of the term. There is no self-analysis by the student. It is my rating which we discuss. I find it hard to help the student to analyze himself and his teaching. I ask him for no written analyses of my teaching or of his own."

2. "I write a daily report of the work of the student in duplicate. The student gets one copy and I keep the other. This written report takes up personal matters as well as teaching. I try to have the student regard the successively daily reports as a 'progress journal.' I find this plan quite successful. We have no self-analysis by the student teacher."

3. "It depends upon the student teacher as to how I take up this problem. Generally I start with teaching results. If qualities of personality or deficiency of preparation by the student are the fault I proceed by carefully directed questions from the teaching results to the weak spot. In some cases I go at once to the weak spot. Both the student teacher and I watch the reactions of the children. For general criticisms I keep a general notebook on my desk in which I write from time to time through the day. Each student looks at this record at noon and at night, making such notes as he wishes. I make duplicate copies of criticisms which are more individual and personal. The student keeps one and I keep the other. Later the student hands his to the director of training who keeps it as a record of the growth of the student teacher."

4. "The student teacher rates himself three times during the term, using the form used by all the city teachers. I ask him to report in writing each day his objectives for himself for that day. At the end of each week he hands to me a written report of accomplishments for the week. This report is an analysis of his teaching and his own growth. In a conference we discuss this report and plan some definite things for the week following. I try to encourage each student teacher."

5. "I am very frank in handling this problem. The student knows that he is to be well prepared and that the children are to make progress. We start right there. We analyze the work of the children and then search for the causes of the shortcomings."

6. "I try to help the student to grow in the ability to criticize himself and his teaching by writing analyses of his teaching, using as the basis for these analyses the progress which the children are making."

7. "If the lesson is going bad, I let it go. Then the student analyzes his teaching. Usually he is able to put his finger on the weak spot. If he cannot, I tell him what is wrong. Then I do pattern teaching, having him analyze in writing what I have done. Following this he plans and teaches. I find it harder to analyze qualities of personality. As a rule if the student is growing in ability to teach he is developing personality also."

8. "I want the student to learn to analyze himself and his teaching and to come to see both his strong and his weak points. I ask him what he is doing each month for himself and what purposes lie back of what he is doing. We work out a list of things which he wants to accomplish and we aim directly at a few of the simpler ones first. We do not attempt too much at a time as it is essential that progress be made. As time goes on we add to the list of things to be accomplished. The student must check

himself to see the progress which he is making. I also ask the student to analyze in writing each lesson he teaches before coming to see me for a conference. We then compare and the student has to decide what is to be done."

9. "I ask the student to recall teachers whom he knows well and thinks are good. What qualities have they which he lacks? What qualities have they which he should seek to acquire? How can he acquire these qualities? Whenever I see improvement in these qualities I tell him so. We use this method in dealing with qualities of teaching and of personality."

10. "I urge the student to keep asking himself the question, Why do I do as I do? Whenever he wants me to demonstrate a procedure which will illustrate a psychological principle that is troubling him I do so. The work begins with demonstration, of course, and I ask the student to try to see not only the procedures used but the principles underlying the procedures. I do not need to spend much time on personality. A genuine interest on my part in the student and in his teaching soon kindles in him a genuine interest in teaching. When this is done the personality practically takes care of itself."

11. "I ask the student to criticize himself and his work. At first he is not very successful in doing this. He increases in ability to analyze as we work together."

12. "We have a rating sheet but I do not make much use of it at first. I try to stimulate the student to raise questions about my teaching and about his own. I feel that my chief task is to make him feel that he must have questions. He evaluates his teaching and so do I. We compare in conference. The student teacher likes to do this and he is ready to see his faults. We use the rating sheet in the same way. If the student over- or underrates himself I try to have an illustration which helps him in defining his judgment."

13. "I make little use of our rating sheet. The student and I spend a great deal of time analyzing teaching, both his and mine. This is a wholly coöperative piece of work and we each make suggestions to the other."

14. "The student rates himself on the rating sheet and so do I. Then we compare our ratings. I find that the student wants to know the points wherein he is weak. He coöperates well and with respect to suggestions relating both to teaching and improvement of personality."

15. "I ask the student teacher to make many informal objective tests so that he may know just what results he is getting. This gives him an objective basis to use in learning to analyze his teaching. This method makes it rather easy to help the student learn to analyze and evaluate teaching. Analysis of personality is difficult for me. I feel that I cannot tell him that certain qualities in his personality are undesirable. I can tell him, however, what qualities in his personality are desirable. I feel that my students make more growth in teaching than in personality."

16. "The three personal qualities which I try to help the student develop are coöperation, leadership, and initiative. I try to create between the student teacher and myself such a relation that the student feels that the classroom is his. Of course, he knows that he must coöperate with me and

the children. I find that the student who develops qualities of leadership and initiative also coöperates well. We both analyze the teaching whether it is his or mine. We use the plan as the starting point and analyze the teaching from the standpoint of the plan."

17. "I ask the student to list the qualities belonging to a good personality and to check the ones in which he feels he is lacking. Then we try to develop those. We study the teaching in much the same way. I ask the student to check his own teaching. He then compares his checking by conferring with me. In this I want him to take the initiative and to raise questions about the teaching procedures which he thinks may be wrong."

The conduct of the conference:

1. "We hold our group conferences twice a week. We take up topics which will help the students with the problems that seem to be giving the most trouble. Discipline, the teaching of reading, language, art, and music are typical topics. I assign readings and the students report what they read, trying especially to relate what they read to the particular problem which we are discussing. The individual conferences are held daily. They are shorter and the problems taken up are individual and personal."

2. "We have two group conferences a week. We have reports of assigned readings. These readings relate generally to the teaching of the subject which the students are going to teach next. This program cannot be followed for every student because not all teach the same subject at the same time so we try to consider the needs of the larger number. The individual conferences are not regularly scheduled. They are held depending upon the individual student's needs. I try to leave the content and time of holding the individual conference to the individual student teacher."

3. "I leave the responsibility for the content of both the group and individual conferences largely to the student teachers. They have their notes taken from our general notebook and their copy of the individual criticisms. As a rule these furnish enough for our conferences. I ask the students to raise their questions first. Generally they are able to discover the issues which we need to discuss. We always have our program for the next week to plan. I want each one to feel free to make suggestions for this program. The individual criticism copy helps the student to determine whether he needs an individual conference with me or not."

4. "I regard the conferences as very important and I prepare very carefully for them. At the group conference we consider general topics in which all are interested. Such topics as general management in the halls, attitude of teacher towards child, and attitude of child towards his work are taken up. In the individual conferences I discuss with the student his teaching and little habits and individual lacks which are interfering with his growth as a teacher."

5. "I hold both group and individual conferences. I find that students regard the conferences as very valuable. They bring general questions to the group conferences and we settle them as a group."

6. "In our group conference we decide what pupil changes we are to work for. This involves a study of the interests, needs, and abilities of

each child. I ask each student to be ready with his opinion as to what pupil changes we should try to make. I ask him to have objective evidence for his opinion. After we have jointly determined the aims for our work we decide what subject matter we shall use to accomplish these aims. In the individual conference I try to give the student the help he needs. I ask the student to bring to the individual conference the things with which he wants help. I generally find that he knows fairly well what his troubles are."

7. "I give more attention to the group than to the individual conferences. If I can succeed in bringing our group conferences up to a high level I find that a formal individual conference is often not necessary. Of course, the individual student teacher has the opportunity for a short conference each day."

8. "We have both group and individual conferences. In the group conferences we consider general problems relating to the management of the classroom, selection and organization of teaching materials, and study of the children. In the individual conferences we consider the student's teaching."

9. "I give more attention to the individual than to the group conferences. I hold an individual conference each day with the student in which we talk about the children, the teaching materials, and the teaching. I also take up with the student questions of personality. In the group conferences we consider general problems such as discipline, management, and decoration of the classroom. I encourage the student teachers to discuss their problems with one another."

10. "Our conferences, both group and individual, are given over to a discussion of the points which the student teachers record in their notebooks from day to day. The notebook is really a register of the student teacher's activities for each day. A typical notebook will have in it a report of the way we have handled such activities as the following: (*a*) Adjusting seats to fit the children; (*b*) making the daily program; (*c*) standards for time allotment; (*d*) study of the course of study; (*e*) study of the attendance record as required by the state register; (*f*) selected bibliography for teachers; (*g*) lists of children's books for class and supplementary reading; (*h*) outlines of method for teaching long division, division of fractions, spelling, and other types of skills; (*i*) diagnostic progress charts for children; (*j*) case studies of children covering such points as attitude towards school, teachers, classmates, and home; (*k*) informal objective tests."

11. "I find the group conference more satisfactory than the individual. Of course, personal problems are best handled in individual conferences. In the group conference I find that the student teachers stimulate thinking on the part of one another."

12. "I hold a group conference at the close of each day. We talk over the problems of the day and the immediate needs which we must take care of the day following and plans are made for the work of the day following. Students feel free to ask for demonstration of the way I handle certain teaching difficulties. Our aim is a complete understanding of the teacher's

work. There is not much need for individual conferences as the group conferences take care of our problems."

13. "Our conferences are really a course in the technique of teaching. We study the children with a view to learning their interests, needs, and abilities. This is done by examining tests which we have given the children. Then we take up the selection and organization of appropriate subject matter to meet these needs, interests, and abilities. Our aim with the children is real learning and for ourselves professional growth. We try to provide the children with a unified school experience. I have but two student teachers at a time so there is not much need for separate conferences."

14. "I hold both group and individual conferences, more of the former than of the latter. In the group conferences we study the teaching, the needs and interests of the children, and the necessary subject matter. I take up the personal problems in the individual conference."

15. "I find that group conferences have the greater value. We learn from one another and the discussions tend to be more objective. We all see what each one does so we all know each other's problems. Each student feels his responsibility for making the conferences successful. I hold an individual conference only when necessary. Not many are necessary."

16. "I am interested in each student becoming the best possible teacher and so I spend a great deal of time analyzing and evaluating the teaching of the individual student teacher. For this reason I emphasize the individual conference rather than the group. Our discussion in the group conferences is rather general."

17. "I do not want any student to become too self-conscious so all personal problems are taken up in the individual conferences. I try to see what are the chief deficiencies of the student and then he and I plan ways of remedying them. Our conferences, for the most part, are group conferences. We all see one another teach and the group can solve nearly every difficulty. Our aim is to keep at a difficulty until we have a solution which is based on sound psychological principles. We test every plan made from the standpoint of the children's interests and needs. We hold our group conference every day."

II. Techniques Reported by Group II

The techniques reported, together with the corresponding activities, are as follows:

1. *Direct student teacher to study children as individuals* (I-5)[a]

Direct student teacher to select, for special observation, one or two children who particularly appeal to him. Direct student to keep record of items of behavior of these children which seem significant. These should be both desirable and undesirable. Discuss these items of behavior to see wherein their significance lies. Help student to analyze conditions which might give rise to this behavior.

[a] The numbers in parentheses refer to section and activity numbers of check list. This is the fifth activity in Section I. See Appendix A, p. 80.

Direct student to continue keeping records, gradually helping him to become alert to each child's particular interests, his personal characteristics, his characteristic reactions, and the desirability of these reactions in the light of that child's particular problems and the efficacy of his adjustment. Help student to see the relation of his home environment, his companions, etc., to his behavior. When the student has become alert to these factors for one or two children help him to analyze others in the same way.

Help student to see the function of the teacher, in the light of such analysis, in helping the child to meet his individual problems more efficiently, through providing conditions for growth for that individual child.

2. *Direct student teacher to study interests of children* (I-13)

Assign reference reading which deals with common interests of children at various stages of development and with reports of studies of special interests of children. Discuss his reading with student teacher until he comes to see the difference between general and special interests of children and to understand the significance of children's interests as a basis for the school program.

Give student the opportunity to study likes and dislikes of children in the training school through (1) observing their reactions to the various school subjects, (2) casual conversations with children, (3) observing them at play at school, (4) observing their work and play at home, (5) interviewing parents, (6) interviewing former teachers, and (7) experimenting by giving children various kinds of work and watching their reactions.

Discuss with student teacher the results of his study of interests common to groups observed and of special interests of individuals and direct him to observe use made of these interests by the school.

3. *Teach student teacher to make an analysis of himself as a prospective teacher* (II-3)

Two techniques were submitted for this activity and since they differ both are reported.

a. I like to help a student teacher to become aware of important points that are most often checked by superintendents and principals. When a teaching position for next year is offered the student, I ask him to make a diagnosis of himself from the standpoint of the position in question. As a guide I refer him to different rating scales used by superintendents and principals. If we are so fortunate as to have several weeks of school left this experience opens the eyes of the student to many very definite things which he wants to learn to do in connection with his work as a student teacher.

b. Soon after the term opens all of the students teaching under my supervision meet with me in group conference. Each student is given the rating card used by all supervisors in the college in grading student teachers. This card lists the following points:

I. Personal equipment

 1. Appearance
 2. Voice
 3. Courtesy
 4. Dependability
 5. Openmindedness

 6. Forcefulness
 7. Resourcefulness
 8. Use of English
 9. Knowledge
 10. Professional habits
  a. Coöperation
  b. Ability in self-criticism

II. Teaching technique

 1. Attention to physical features
 2. Care of material
 3. Preparation and organization of subject matter
 4. Skill in
  a. Arousing and holding interest
  b. Stimulating pupil activity
  c. Questioning
  d. Use of illustrative material
  e. Recognizing and providing for individual differences
  f. Preparing and using drill material
  g. Review
  h. Testing and grading
 5. Ability to control
 6. Pupil achievement
  a. Knowledge and skills
  b. Desirable habits and attitudes

All points are discussed in the group conference. I try to show the extent to which all points can or cannot be measured and my interpretation of them as related to the particular school grade which these students are teaching. Students are interested at the beginning because they know that this is the card used in reporting the term grade in student teaching to the director of training. Each student is encouraged to observe different supervisors and, also, other student teachers teaching the same class section as he is teaching and to criticise his own technique, the pupils' reaction to him, and the results he obtains.

Each student is asked to rate himself with this card and bring it to private conference with me at the middle of the term. Students are told to criticise themselves fairly, to select their good points as well as their bad points and not to under-estimate or overestimate their work. If they are not able to criticise their own teaching and select the good from the bad, they cannot know whether to continue any procedure they have tried. This discussion tends to cause the student to make a conscientious effort to evaluate his teaching as he should.

When the student brings his card at the middle of the term, I have a card, also, on which I have marked a rating. We compare the cards and discuss the differences.

4. *Direct student teacher in study of qualities making up best teaching personality* (II-14)

Refer student teacher to studies or lists of personality traits that are considered essential to teaching success. Using these studies or lists the student makes a self-rating scale and evaluates his own personality traits.

The supervisor, using the same scale which the student has made, also rates the student. Following this the supervisor and student compare their ratings and discuss their reasons for the differences.

The student indicates the points in which he wishes to improve. The supervisor, so far as possible, gives the student teacher activities to perform that will call into play the traits in which the student wants improvement.

5. *Help student teacher to develop professional attitudes* (II-29)

Discuss with student and assign readings on the values and responsibilities of the work of teaching, its rewards and satisfactions. Give the student teacher duties of gradually increasing responsibility so that he will be enabled to derive satisfaction from their successful performance. Discuss with student the strong points of the school he is attending and of its administration.

Lead the student to make personal sacrifices to further his teaching work and endeavor to see that satisfaction in the way of self-approval for having done so follows. Help the student to plan independent study contributing to his efficiency in teaching and encourage him to carry it through. Endeavor to have the student become a member of the local teachers' organization, attend regularly, and participate.

Draw the student into and encourage discussion of educational problems with others. Hold meetings of student teachers and training school faculty to which student teachers contribute solution of problems of organization and management as they are capable.

Discuss with the student teacher and encourage him to plan for graduate study in his particular field of teaching. Encourage and recognize efforts of the student teacher to gain new professional information. Have student teachers arrange and have charge of displays of school work which represent the work of their pupils. Talk happily of the work of teaching in student conferences and encourage a joyous attitude toward teaching.

6. *Give student teacher outline to guide his observations* (II-42)

Observation outline: The student teacher is first asked to look over the points in the outline. When in the classroom the student is to make a diary record of the whole situation, reporting the facts as suggested by the outline. Different reports may be limited to parts of the outline.

I. Physical conditions of classroom
   A. Hygienic conditions
      1. Lighting
      2. Ventilation
      3. Temperature
      4. Cleanliness
      5. Seating

B. Equipment
  1. Furniture, blackboard, materials
    a. On hand
    b. Needed
    c. How placed

C. Appearance
  1. Decorations
    a. Permanent
    b. Temporary
  2. Home atmosphere

II. Work of the classroom
  A. Social factors
    1. The teacher
      a. Appearance
      b. Voice
      c. Poise
      d. Sympathy
      e. Attitude toward work
      f. English
      g. Health
    2. The children
      a. Coöperation with teacher
      b. Coöperation with one another
      c. Joy in school activities
      d. Passive or active participation
    3. Order in the classroom
      a. Group control
        (1) By teacher
        (2) By pupils
    4. Habit formation
      a. Obedience
      b. Responsibility
      c. Industry
      d. Initiative
      e. Self-dependence
      f. Courtesy

  B. Routine factors
    1. Organization of room procedure
      a. Economy of time in
        (1) Calling and dismissing classes
        (2) Handling of materials
      b. Economy of materials by
        (1) Teacher
        (2) Children
    2. Daily program
      a. Balance maintained between
        (1) Physical and mental activity
        (2) Individual and group activity
        (3) Pupil and teacher activity

III. Subject matter
    A. Selection
        1. With reference to pupil experiences, interests, and capacities
        2. With reference to social values

    B. Organization
        1. In large units or topics commonly providing for pupil projects
        2. In terms which learner can understand
        3. Providing for progressive sequence
        4. Providing for helpful correlation

    C. Presentation of subject matter
        1. Recitation
            a. Aim of teacher and pupils
                (1) Appropriateness
                (2) Definiteness
            b. Method in terms of types of learning
                (1) Association of ideas
                (2) Motor
                (3) Drill
                (4) Problem solving
                (5) Expression
                (6) Enjoyment
            c. Teaching technique
                (1) Well-prepared plans
                (2) Ability to meet emergencies
                (3) Skill in questioning and in directing discussion
                (4) Attention to individual needs
            d. Achievements and results
                (1) Maximum activity by all pupils, such as information, thinking, acquiring skill, establishing associations, moral behavior
        2. Seat work
            a. Selected by teacher or pupil
            b. Purposeful, definite, absorbing
            c. Degree of independence and initiative shown
            d. Related to other school activities
            e. Results checked

IV. Provision for individual differences
    A. Classification
    B. Management of different groups
    C. Group and individual work
        1. Superior children
        2. Retarded children

7. Tell student teacher of valuable references (II-49)

To do this the supervisor must have a catalogued and annotated bibliography of helpful teaching materials and methods. This can be built up by reviewing all reports and studies of teaching materials and methods—both books and articles—that have been published dealing with the teacher's work. This bibliography must be kept up to date by continuous reading.

8. *Teach student teacher to make lesson plans* (III-1)

Discuss with the student teacher the need for planning lessons, work, and activities in any business or profession. Have student observe evidences of planning in life situations, looking for evidences of not planning and the consequences. Have the student read references on planning lessons or activities.

Teach a demonstration lesson for the student. Discuss with the student the plan of the lesson observed, how it was made, teacher's part and child's part in the plan, and the form used.

Teach another lesson for the student in which teacher and children together make a plan. The student teacher takes full notes, writes out the plan for the lesson, and then discusses plan with teacher. The student studies other kinds of plans and ways of making them for various kinds of lessons.

The student takes charge of the part of the lesson where planning new work begins and plans work with the children for the next day. He writes this plan out in detail and discusses it with the teacher. He teaches the lesson according to the plan.

The student teaches and plans each day's work with the children's help. He writes plans for all lessons in some detail until various kinds of activities are cared for and until certain steps in planning them are habitual. When this degree of attainment has been reached the written plan is shortened to a form that is practical for use in public school situations.

9. *Help student teacher in planning units of work* (III-20)

Direct the student teacher to study the child activity evidenced in the classroom as well as the curriculum requirements. Select a topic from the children's activity which is of vital interest to the children and which will satisfy the curriculum requirements. Direct the student teacher to organize valuable available subject matter and illustrative material around the topic. Before this organization of the subject matter is made I suggest the selection of the major divisions under which the minor ones are to be grouped, emphasizing that the selection and elimination of subject matter be made all in view of the children's interests, needs, and capacities. In this work, the curriculum cannot be ignored under the present scheme of things.

10. *Teach demonstration lessons for student teacher* (III-28)

Decide with the student what type of demonstration will be most helpful. Plan with the children so that the lesson desired will fit in with their needs as far as possible. Plan the lesson with the student's help, stating principles, bibliography, and method. Write the plan out in detail and put copy into student's hands. Have student become familiar with it and the references on the subject. Have student suggest improvements or criticise it.

With the student's assistance make out a set of questions which the lesson hopes to answer. Teach the lesson planned. The student observes to answer the definite questions. Discuss the lesson taught with the student, keeping in mind the problems. Encourage suggestions, criticisms, and comments from the student.

11. *Teach student teacher to use standardized tests in connection with his teaching* (III-41)

The supervisor has a file of several of each type of the best standardized tests suitable for use in her grade. This file is available to the student teachers who are asked to familiarize themselves with the various tests so that they can discuss them in conference. In connection with this study of the tests the students should do some reading to find out the value and limitations of tests.

The students and supervisor then hold a conference in which they discuss tests as to kinds, use, and value. A set of criteria for the judgment of tests is worked out, some of which will probably be as follows:

a. Does the test measure what it is claimed to measure?
b. Is it comprehensive and long enough to be an accurate measure?
c. Is it easily scored?
d. Does it have definite directions for administering?
e. Does it have definite directions for scoring?
f. Are the directions for the children clear?
g. Is the test reliable?
h. Are there well-established norms?
i. Are there charts and tables which enable the teacher to interpret the scores?

With these criteria in mind each student teacher selects the test which he thinks is suitable to use for diagnostic testing purposes. The supervisor directs the students to give special study to the test chosen in regard to administering and scoring and to be ready to give the test.

At the next conference the supervisor explains and demonstrates timing of test giving, making clear that the examiner must use a watch with a second hand. The supervisor also explains the importance of a well-modulated but clear voice on the part of the examiner and the necessity for providing the most favorable physical conditions for the children. Then each student gives a test or part of a test to the others in the group. Suggestions are then made to the student of points which he needs to watch more carefully. The method of scoring is then explained and each student scores one of each type of test and checks the work of another student.

The tests are then given to the pupils by the student teacher under regular laboratory conditions. Each student scores the tests he gave and tabulates the results. The scoring and tabulating are checked to insure no errors.

At the next conference the supervisor directs the discussion of the use of the test results to include these points:

a. Use of test scores for diagnostic purposes.
b. Comparison of individual scores with class score and with grade norm.
c. Making graphs and charts to show the achievement made by each child.
d. Planning the work to take care of the needs of each child.

12. *Teach student teacher to see the principles for caring for the physical conditions of the classroom* (IV-8)

For the first few days that the student teacher is with me I attend to all the physical conditions of the classroom myself. Finally I decide that he now knows that this is one of the most important duties of the teacher and that he should take over this work. I plan that he will find me arranging the shades so as to give the best lighting conditions when he comes to the classroom the next day. I ask him to help, telling him to notice the differences in the amount of light in different parts of the classroom with the shades poorly arranged. At our next conference we discuss proper temperature, ventilation, and lighting for school rooms. I show the student how these things are controlled in our classroom and I tell him all that I have actually done that day so as to provide the best conditions for the pupils.

I assign readings which discuss the principles underlying caring for physical conditions of the classroom. I ask the student to observe many classrooms and note how the physical conditions are cared for. Soon he finds some in which they are not properly cared for. I ask him to note the children at work in such classrooms. This gives him a basis for appreciating the principles set forth in the reading assigned.

I have had student teachers who regard caring for physical conditions of the classroom as beneath them. When I show them that I do it and how necessary it is they soon come to have a high standard of attainment with respect to such things.

13. *Hold individual conferences with student teacher each week* (V-22)

The student teacher and supervisor set a time for the regular weekly conference period which is convenient to both. At the first conference the student and supervisor agree upon the standards for judging teaching procedures and decide that the chief responsibility for the content of the conference discussion rests upon the student.

The student regards the conference as his opportunity to discuss in detail with an experienced teacher who knows the children with whom he is working all problems which are troubling him. He brings to the conference problems regarding the children, selection and organization of materials, planning of lessons, teaching, and management. He proposes the methods which he wants to use in solving these problems, basing his suggestions on ideas gained from his work both in the college and in the training school. He analyzes his teaching procedures of the previous week with a view to discovering wherein they were faulty. He asks for demonstration lessons to illustrate the application of principles.

The work of the supervisor is chiefly that of adviser. To call the student's attention to problems which are being overlooked, the supervisor develops rather than tells.

F

BIBLIOGRAPHY

ALLEN, C. R. *The Instructor, the Man and the Job.* J. B. Lippincott Company, Philadelphia, 1912.

ANDERSON, C. J., BARR, A. S. and BUSH, M. G. *Visiting the Teacher at Work.* D. Appleton and Company, 1925.

ARMENTROUT, W. D. *The Conduct of Student Teaching in State Teachers Colleges.* Greeley, Colorado, 1927.

ARMENTROUT, W. D. "Making Observation Effective for Teachers in Training." *Educational Administration and Supervision,* 10: 287-293.

AVENT, J. E. *Beginning Teaching.* Published by Author, Knoxville, Tennessee, 1926.

AYER, F. C. and BARR, A. S. *The Organization of Supervision.* D. Appleton and Company, New York, 1928.

BAGLEY, WILLIAM C. and KEITH, JOHN A. *An Introduction to Teaching.* The Macmillan Company, 1924.

BARR, A. S. and BURTON, W. H. *The Supervision of Instruction.* D. Appleton and Company, New York, 1926.

BLACKHURST, J. H. *Directed Observation and Supervised Teaching.* Ginn & Company, Boston, 1925.

BODE, BOYD. "Principles of Curriculum Construction." *Educational Administration and Supervision,* 12: 217-228.

BOBBITT, J. FRANKLIN. *How to Make a Curriculum.* Houghton Mifflin Company, Boston, 1924.

BONSER, F. G. *The Elementary School Curriculum.* The Macmillan Company, New York, 1924.

BONSER, F. G. "The Training of Teachers for the New Education." *Progressive Education,* April-May-June, 1929, Vol. VI, No. 2, pp. 111-121.

CHARTERS, W. W. and WAPLES, D. *The Commonwealth Teacher-Training Study.* University of Chicago Press, Chicago, 1929.

CHARTERS, W. W. and WHITLEY, I. B. *Analysis of Secretarial Duties and Traits.* Williams and Wilkins, Baltimore, 1924.

CHARTERS, W. W. "Inadequacy of Principles of Teaching." *Educational Administration and Supervision,* 4: 215-221.

CHARTERS, W. W. "Principles Underlying the Making of the Curriculum of Teacher-Training Institutions." *Educational Administration and Supervision,* 10: 337-346.

COLLINGS, E. "The Meaning and Function of Creative Supervision." *Journal of Educational Method,* 4: 404-409.

DOUGLASS, AUBREY A. *Secondary Education.* Houghton Mifflin Company, Boston, 1927.

FRASIER, G. W. and ARMENTROUT, W. D. *An Introduction to Education.* Scott, Foresman and Company, Chicago, 1924.

GARRISON, NOBLE LEE. *Status and Work of the Training Supervisor.* Teachers College, Columbia University. Contributions to Education, No. 280, 1927.

LEARNED, W. S., BAGLEY, W. C. and others. *The Professional Preparation of Teachers for American Public Schools.* Bulletin 14, 1920. New York, The Carnegie Foundation for the Advancement of Teaching.

MILLER, H. L. "University of Wisconsin Plan for Preparation of High School Teachers." *Eighteenth Year Book, Part I, National Society for Study of Education,* pp. 7-165. Public School Publishing Company, Bloomington, 1919.

MINOR, RUBY. *Principles of Teaching Practically Applied.* Houghton Mifflin Company, Boston, 1924.

MYERS, A. F. and BEECHEL, E. F. *Manual of Observation and Participation.* American Book Company, New York, 1926.

NUTT, H. W. *Current Problems in the Supervision of Instruction.* Johnson Publishing Company, Richmond, 1928.

NUTT, H. W. "A Fundamental Weakness in Teacher-Training Courses." *Educational Administration and Supervision,* 12 : 200-203.

PARKER, S. C. *Types of Learning and Teaching.* Ginn and Company, Boston, 1925.

PARKER, S. C. *General Methods of Teaching in the Elementary School.* Ginn and Company, Boston, 1919.

PENDLETON, C. S. "The Content and Method of Subject Matter Courses in Teachers Colleges." *Peabody Journal of Education,* 3 :273-292.

PRYOR, H. C. "Graded Exercises in Practice Teaching." *Educational Administration and Supervision,* 5 : 411-422.

RANDOLPH, E. D. *The Professional Treatment of Subject Matter.* Warwick and York, Baltimore, 1924.

RUSSELL, CHARLES. *The Improvement of the City Elementary School Teacher in Service.* Teachers College, Columbia University, Contributions to Education, No. 128, 1922.

SHONINGER, Y. S. "Function and Responsibilities of the Critic Teacher." *Educational Administration and Supervision,* 6 : 481-490.

SNEDDEN, D. "Job Analysis, Needed Foundations of Teacher Training." *Educational Administration and Supervision,* 10 : 30-36.

STRONG, E. K. and UHRBROCK, R. S. *Job Analysis and the Curriculum.* Williams and Wilkins, Baltimore, 1923.

THOMAS, FRANK W. *Principles and Technique of Teaching.* Houghton Mifflin Company, Boston, 1927.

UHL, WILLIS L. *The Supervision of Secondary Subjects.* D. Appleton and Company, New York, 1929.

UHLER, J. M. *A Partial Analysis of the Duties of the Critic Teacher.* Master's Thesis, University of Pittsburgh, 1928.